I Saw Them Die

Diary and Recollections of Shirley Millard

---

by Shirley Millard

edited by Adele Comandini

---

with 2011 Foreword
by Elizabeth Townsend Gard

Quid Pro Books

New Orleans, Louisiana

I Saw Them Die

Compilation and Foreword copyright © 2011 by Elizabeth Townsend Gard. All rights reserved. No copyright is claimed in the original text. The source work was originally published in 1936 by Harcourt, Brace & Company, Inc. (New York).

Published in the 2011 edition by Quid Pro Books.

Quid Pro, LLC
5860 Citrus Blvd., Suite D-101
New Orleans, Louisiana 70123
www.quidprobooks.com

ISBN: 9781610270236
ISBN-10: 1610270231

ꟼP

Publisher's Cataloging-in-Publication

Millard, Shirley.

I saw them die: diary and recollections of Shirley Millard / by Shirley Millard.

Edited in 1936 edition by Adele Comandini.

2011 Foreword by Elizabeth Townsend Gard.

p. cm.

Includes Foreword and Editors' Notes.

Series: *Journeys and Memoirs.*

ISBN: 9781610270236 (pbk)
ISBN: 9781610270229 (ePub)
ISBN: 9780982750445 (Kindle)

"An unprepared nurse from the United States volunteering in World War I France shares her diary and later reflections of the horrific and poignant events of 1918, and in the process reveals more about the fascinating people and times, and especially herself, than she apparently realized even in writing it. Presented to modern readers with a new Foreword by law professor and historian Elizabeth Townsend Gard, and featuring representative photographs of the era."

1. History—World War I. 2. History—Red Cross. 3. World War, 1914-1918— Personal narratives. 4. History—Nursing. I. Title. II. Series.

CONTENTS

Note by the Series Editor..i

2011 Foreword..iii

Photographs...xi

Editor's Note...xxi

Author's Foreword...xxiii

I Saw Them Die

    I..1

    II...5

    III...11

    IV..15

    V..21

    VI..31

    VII...39

    VIII..45

    IX..53

    X..63

About the 2011 Edition..69

Note by the Series Editor
from the 2011 edition

This book is the true contemporary account of an American volunteer nurse's horrific—and and sometimes bizarre—experiences while serving at a French battlefield hospital near Soissons during World War I. It has poignant layers which even the often-naïve author did not find in her own crisp prose. "As our *camion* drove through the château gate we could see that the grounds were covered with what looked like sleeping men." That is just her own introduction to the unit, housed in what was once a stately country estate, and soon she was standing hours on end treating friend and enemy alike, facing harrowing hyperreality with aplomb.

Shirley Millard is throughout a willing reporter of her fascinating perspective on war, youth, loss, and love—and always slapdash surgery and gallows camaraderie, inside a MASH unit before there was *M*A*S*H*. And before antibiotics, it is painfully clear.

But she is also an unwitting reporter of so much more. The modern reader sees truths and wrongs that Shirley fails to experience herself, some at the time and too many upon her rested reflection. Even some of the simple pronouns she uses startle today's reader, and reveal the author and the understory more than she ever realized. The book compels attention not only on the level on which she wrote it, which would be plenty enough to bring crashing home this forgotten war, but also on levels she did not intend. Either way the insights pierce through, as when the young French doctor sums up war: *"La gloire, la gloire! Bah! C'est de la merde!"* He is an unmitigated hero too, but is revealed in his own incongruous scenes later, just in his smoking habits alone.

This collection of diary entries and later flashbacks inevitably draws comparison as a personal account of World War I to that of the much more self-aware Erich Remarque (though readers here may find themselves drawn into the lack of awareness as much as the account itself). Yet this book seems to have been lost in time and the crush of later events—more war to come, human atrocities by German scientists in concentration camps, pacifism, too many men ruined to be able to "process" in any sense of that word. Stunningly, many of these historic events Shirley herself actually *foreshadowed* in places that are accidentally embedded with the reality that the world later lived, soon after this book was written. She witnessed a lifetime in her brave volunteer work in France in 1918, and she even wrote words having, again without realizing it, ominous import to lifetimes to come.

One is tempted to ask *what would have happened if Paris Hilton went to M*A*S*H and wrote a diary about it*. But that does not quite capture the depth of the book, the true heroism of the author, or the brilliant prose she shares. The utter incongruity of it all—the events of the time, the later drawing room reflection—makes the account more than just a Hollywood pitch line in the elevator. Even so, the reader will be forgiven for asking the Paris question. Reading this book becomes like an Easter egg hunt for moments of unreflected twist and irony (when are maggots *good* news? why not "him"? watermelon seeds?). These moments do feel much like there is some truth to the elevator pitch.

One person who studied in-depth these layers and incongruities, as part of original research for her Ph.D. in Modern European History from the University of California at Los Angeles (1998), was Professor Elizabeth Townsend Gard. She offers her own account of the account, as the contemporary Foreword to this edition.

In her introduction, Townsend Gard explores the book's history and themes, and its particular backstory. She places it in the war genre of the times and relates it to more famous work of other writers, poets, and artists of the era. Quid Pro is proud to offer this introduction, and the original work, as part of the *Journeys and Memoirs Series*. I personally thank her for bringing this book back to scholarly and popular attention, and for writing her much more global Foreword to introduce it and position it within a literary tradition, and a feminist one as well.

Steven Alan Childress
Conrad Meyer III Professor of Law,
Tulane University
For QUID PRO BOOKS

New Orleans, Louisiana
March 2011

2011 FOREWORD

I first encountered Shirley Millard's *I Saw Them Die* when I was working on my dissertation in the early 1990s. At the time, there were few well known or remembered World War I works written by women, and I was on a quest to find whether women wrote and what they had written about. Dialing into individual library catalogs—before the advent of the Internet—I found over 500 books by 300 authors. Shirley Millard's book was among one I found. Upon reading the 1936 work, it became one of my favorites, for it exemplified many of the themes and styles I was finding. I began to assign the book to students as well as to include the women's story in a way that complemented works like Remarque's *All Quiet on the Western Front*.

As time passed, a renaissance of women's war writings occurred. Not only were Vera Brittain's works republished—*someone* had remained famous with regard to her writings about war—but many other "new" voices began to appear. Among them, Irene Rathbone and Helen Z. Smith gained some attention. Millard's book, however, has remained nearly forgotten. I hope others find it useful and enjoyable, as I did.

An Introduction to the War Generation

> We know only that in some strange and melancholy way we have become a waste land. At the same time, we are not often sad.
>
> Erich Maria Remarque
> *All Quiet on the Western Front* (1929)[1]

By 1936, the First World War had been over for almost two decades. Unlike the more famous war generation writers, we have little information about Millard beyond the work itself. But she fits within the profile of the war generation, and this is what makes her writing so fascinating—an untapped gem. She echoes the themes we see in the works of Vera Brittain, Siegfried Sassoon, Robert Graves, Irene Rathbone, and so many others. Her work is indicative of the prevalence of the themes we see with World War I and the young people who went to war and believed in the cause.

---

[1] Erich Maria Remarque, *All Quiet on the Western Front*, translated from the German by A.W. Wheen (orig. 1929, rpt. New York: Fawcett Crest, 1987), 19.

Her work was published in 1936. Millard writes that she found her war diaries while packing for a move. It is not terribly surprising she would have had the idea of publishing "her version." By the mid-1930s, the literary canon of the First World War literature had already been firmly established. The stories of war as told from those men and women who had been there had become its own genre.

Within the seven-year period of 1926-1933, the genre developed.[2] Written primarily by participants born in the late 1880s and 1890s, these works continue today to stand as the central literary representation of the experiences of the First World War. Many, including Vera Brittain, had published war-poetry during or just after the war, and for some, like Siegfried Sassoon, Edmund Blunden, and Robert Graves, this brought them early attention.[3] For a good number, however, their major impact on the literary world would come with the publishing of their memoirs and novels ten to fifteen years after the war.[4] Vera Brittain's memoir *Testament of Youth* came at the end of the war-book boom in 1933. Shirley Millard's recollections as *I Saw Them Die* followed three years later.

---

[2] *See* Samuel Hynes, *A War Imagined: The First World War and English Culture* (London: The Bodley Head, 1990), 424-425. How quantitatively significant the war-books were is hard to calculate. John Onions in *English Fiction and Drama of the Great War, 1918-1939* (New York: Palgrave Macmillan, 1990), 49, saw the avalanche of war books beginning in 1927, with the specific date of arrival as the tenth anniversary of the Armistice, November 1928. Using Philip Hager and Desmond Taylor's *The Novels of World War One: An Annotated Bibliography* (1981), Onions counted eight novels in 1927, ten in 1928, twenty-five in 1929, thirty-six in 1930, ten in 1931, and thirteen in 1932. These numbers have always seemed low to me, especially since they only reflect men. Also, the list does not include memoirs, poetry, or plays, three very important categories. Blunden's *Undertones of War*, R.C. Sherriff's *Journey's End: A Play in Three Acts*, Sassoon's memoirs trilogy, and Graves' *Goodbye to All That*, for instance, would not have been included.

[3] In addition, a number of the most prominent war poets from the war generation did not survive the war. Their poetry is included as part of the canonized voice of the war generation. Some of the most famous war poets include Rupert Brookes (1887-1915), Charles Hamilton Sorley (1895-1915), Edward Thomas (1878-1917), Isaac Rosenberg (1890-1918), Wilfred Owen (1893-1918), and Ivor Gurney (1890-1937). For a short selection of their poems, *see* Candace Ward, ed., *World War One British Poets: Brooke, Owen, Sassoon, Rosenberg, and Others* (Mineola, New York: Dover Publications, Inc., 1997). There is also the case of Paul Nash (b. 1889), who received prominence during the second half of the war for his paintings; he survived the war only to paint the Second World War as well.

[4] *See* Samuel Hynes, *A War Imagined*, 424-25.

iv

While the war generation published their experiences of war as memoirs and diaries in the late 1920s and early 1930s, it would be a handful of scholars forty years later that would further canonize their experiences. Paul Fussell, Robert Wohl, and Samuel Hynes are three of the most recognized cultural historians to have defined the First World War and the war generation.[5] What is distinctly missing from all three accounts are voices of women as war generationalists, although Vera Brittain is included in all three studies. (In fact, Wohl and Hynes give her a prominent place in their works.) In good part, this is because most of the women of the war generation were almost completely lost to history, some of the most lost members of their generation. When I began working on my own study in the 1980s, little scholarly material existed about women in war, and in particular, women in the First World War. In 1977, it was still reasonable for Vera Brittain's esteemed daughter Shirley Williams to write in a preface to a new edition of her mother's memoir that *"Testament of Youth* is, I think, the only book about the First World War written by a woman...."[6] This statement was, in part, what motivated me to investigate to indeed see whether other women had written about their experiences during the war.

In the last twenty-five years, anthologies, collections of essays, and scholarly studies specifically focused on women's experiences and writings about the First World War have begun to appear in great numbers. Some focus on the role of women in munitions, poetry by women, organization structures, or propaganda during the war.[7] Others are

---

[5] Paul Fussell, *The Great War and Modern Memory* (Oxford Univ. Press, 25th anniv. ed., 2000); Robert Wohl, *The Generation of 1914* (Harvard Univ. Press, 1981); Hynes, *A War Imagined* (1990).

[6] One of my earliest projects investigated whether this indeed could be true—that Vera Brittain was the only woman to write about the First World War. As noted, my search turned up over 500 works by 300 women.

[7] For munitions work, *see* Deborah Thom, *Nice Girls and Rude Girls: Women Workers in World War I* (London: I.B. Tauris Publishers, 1998); Angela Wollacott, *On Her Their Lives Depend* (University of California Press, 1994); Gareth Griffiths, *Women's Factory Work in World War One* (Sutton Publishers, 1991); Gail Braybon, *Women Workers in the First World War* (Croom Helm, 1981); and Gail Braybon and Penny Summerfield, *Out of the Cage* (Pandora, 1987).

For poetry, *see* Nosheen Khan, *Women's Poetry of the First World War* (Univ. Press of Kentucky, 1988); Joan Montgomery Byles, *War, Women, and Poetry, 1914-1945* (Newark: University of Delaware Press, 1995); and Catherine W. Reilly, ed., *Scars Upon My Heart: Women's Poetry and Verse of the First World War* (London: Virago Press, 1981).

For the homefront, *see* Margaret H. Darrow, *French Women and the First World War: War Stories of the Home Front* (Oxford: Berg, 2000); Susan R.

anthologies of women writing on war, and women writers in war.[8]
Additionally, novels, diaries, and memoirs of women have been, in some
cases, printed for the first time and others, reprinted.[9] Shirley Millard's

---

Grayzel, *Women's Identities at War: Gender, Motherhood, and Politics in
Britain and France During the First World War* (Chapel Hill: University of
North Carolina Press, 1999); Ute Daniel, *The War from Within: German
Working Class Women in the First World War* (New York: Berg, 1997).

For feminist studies, *see* Margaret Randolph Higonnet and Jane Jensen,
eds., *Behind the Lines: Gender and the Two World Wars*, Claire M. Tylee, *The
Great War and Women's Consciousness: Images of Militarism and Woman-
hood in Women's Writings, 1914-64* (University of Iowa Press; 1990); Sharon
Ouditt, *Fighting Forces, Writing Women: Identity and Ideology in the First
World War* (Routledge, 1994); Susan Gilbert and Susan Gubar, *No Man's Land:
the Place of the Woman Writer in the Twentieth Century* (New Haven: Yale
University Press, 1987); and Françoise Thébaud, *Le Femme au Temps de la
Guerre de 14* (Paris: Stock/L. Pernoud, 1986).

For works documenting women's war experiences, *see* Dorothy Schneider
and Carl J. Schneider, *Into the Breach: American Women Overseas in World
War I* (Viking, 1991); Susan Zeiger, *In Uncle Sam's Service: Women Workers
With the American Expeditionary Force, 1917-1919* (Cornell University Press,
2000); Lettie Gavin, *American Women in World War One: They Also Served*
(Univ. Press of Colorado, 1997); and Elaine F. Weiss, *Fruits of Victory: The
Woman's Land Army of America in the Great War* (Potomac Books, Inc, 2008).

For a recent work on Italy, *see* Allison Scardino Belzer, *Women and the
Great War: Femininity Under Fire in Italy* (Palgrave Macmillan, 2010).

[8] For anthologies and collections of essays, *see* Suzanne Raitt and Trudi Tate,
eds., *Women's Fiction and the Great War* (Oxford: Clarendon Press, 1997);
Dorothy Goldman, *Women and World War One: The Written Response* (Mac-
millan, 1993); Agnes Cardinal, Dorothy Goldman, and Judith Hattaway, eds.,
Women's Writing on the First World War (Oxford Univ. Press, 2000); Angela
Smith, ed., *Women's Writing of the First World War* (Manchester Univ. Press,
2000); Nosheen Khan, ed., *Not with Loud Grieving: Women's Verse of the
Great War: An Anthology* (Polymer, 1994); and Joyce Marlow, ed., *The Virago
Book of Women and the Great War* (London: Virago Press, 1999).

For bibliographies, *see* Sharon Ouditt, *First World War Women Writers:
An Annotated Bibliography* (Routledge, 2000); Sigrid Markman and Dagmar
Lange, *Frauen and Erster Weltkrid in England: Auswahlbibliographie* (Osna-
brück: H.th. Wenner., 1988); and Catherine W. Reilly, *English Poetry of the
First World War: A Bibliography* (London: G. Prior, 1978).

For photographs, *see* Diana Condell and Jean Liddiard, *Working for Vic-
tory?: Images of Women in the First World War, 1914-18* (London: Routledge &
Kegan Paul, 1987); and Max Arthur, *The Road Home: The Aftermath of the
Great War Told by the Men and Women Who Survived It* (Phoenix, 2010).

[9] For first time published and republished works, examples include Irene Rathbone, *We That Were Young* (New York: The Feminist Press at the City Uni-

work remains relatively unknown.

Shirley Millard's War

We know very little about Shirley Millard outside of the text. But what we learn from the text is enough. She finds her 1918 diary when she is about to move. She now has a five-year old son. She has a full life, with servants and butter-knives. When she finds herself face-to-face with her 1918 diary, she emerges an hour later, and says to one of her servants, "I am going to write a book." This small introduction mimics many of the themes of the war generation—a diary is kept during the war; fifteen years later, the author reconstructs the experience through narrative; the author is from a privileged class, either upper or upper-middle class; and the writer feels compelled to revisit that time of her life. It is a classic war generation story. So in many ways, we do not care that we do not know more about Shirley Millard, for she stands in the place of so many others who experienced the First World War, and then sought to tell the story of war a decade (and in this case, nearly two decades) later.

What drew me to the work initially was the structure—a diary interspersed with remembrances and narrative. We see in the genre diaries; we see fictional diaries; we see narratives based on diaries. Here we see the blending of both diary and later memory.

Her experiences and narrative of the war begin in 1918, when many of the war generation had finished their story. The war for many had begun in 1914. The Americans came in late. Shirley Millard reflects this. And yet, what is amazing about the account is that the innocence, excitement, and joy of 1914 is still present in 1918—beginnings are beginnings, even four years later. Like Vera Brittain and others, she herself had brothers and friends that had already enlisted. She too wanted to be part of the war effort. "I wanted to go overseas!" (Page 2.)

The themes Millard writes were present in so many war books at the time—an inexperienced girl determined to go an adventure that she would never have dreamed of had there not been work; a girl frustrated with merely sewing or knitting for the cause; a girl wanting to be part of helping, whether driving an ambulance or caring for the dying in France. Even her dreaming of nursing back to health her then-love is something found fairly consistently in these texts.

---

versity of New York, orig. 1932, rpt. 1989); Enid Bagnold, *The Happy Foreigner* (Virago, 1987, orig. 1920); and Helen Zenna Smith, *Not So Quiet: Stepdaughters of the War* (New York: The Feminist Press at the City University of New York, orig. 1930, rpt. 1989).

Like many WWI accounts, Millard's began with the journey to war. The present of a pen for writing love letters, chocolates, and the presence of flowers are familiar objects of youth departing for war. And those writing the story of war were the youth of war—often the youngest participating. This was true also of Robert Graves, Edmund Blunden, and Vera Brittain.

Millard's images of her arrival are also familiar in this genre, and the blend of her excitement at landing and her memories of what happened form a cohesive story usually reserved only for a comparison of two texts—the diary and the later memoir. And then, she begins to gain experience—with long hours, hard living conditions, and the horror of war. Like many writers before her, writing of the horror included writing about prisoners, and she, like Vera Brittain, would soon find that the enemy had mothers, had fears, and were merely children themselves.

She sees much death, and not just from the soldiers. Nurses also die, and are put in danger all the time—sometimes volunteering for ambulance duty or even serving in a field unit, and sometimes the hospital itself must be evacuated. She also experiences romance. Love and death. All part of the experience of war for this generation.

And then she describes the end of war. For many, the end of war came earlier than November 11, 1918, but Shirley is there at the end. Her description is a mixture of sadness, relief, and loss. "Only then did the enormous crime of the whole thing begin to come home to me," she remembers. She wonders as she packed her belongings "and got ready to leave[,] [l]eave for where? Home? I felt a sudden shyness about returning home." (Pp. 65-66.)

In the end, Millard's life looked whole—marrying and having a son—but if she was like the others in the war generation, her experiences and memories of her time in war probably stayed with her and influenced many decisions. She ends the work, "Now the world is once again beating the drums of war. To my son Coco, his friends and their mothers I offer this simple record of the dark caravan that winds endlessly through the memory of my youth." (P. 68.) She, like Vera Brittain, Erich Maria Remarque, and countless others, wanted her experience to mean something—perhaps serve as a warning for another generation on the realities and price of war.

In 1936, the world saw itself headed into war once again. The editor's words that began this book suggests Millard achieved her goal for *I Saw Them Die*: "When Mrs. Millard placed her diary of 1918 in my hands, I had just finished declaring that in spite of my distaste of violence, I could never quite bring myself to embrace the negative philosophies of pacifism. Today I cannot truthfully repeat this assertion. The part I have played in preparing this manuscript from Mrs. Millard's journal and notes has left its mark on me." (P. xxi.)

I am very pleased that Alan Childress suggested the republication of this work. I hope many come to read it and see the gem of a work that it is. Shirley Millard's *I Saw Them Die* should be a classic, along with Vera Brittain's *Testament of Youth* and Erich Maria Remarque's *All Quiet on the Western Front*. The work provides a glimpse into the experience and horror of war in all the language that we now identify as making up the experience of the war generation.

Elizabeth Townsend Gard
Associate Professor of Law,
Tulane University
and
Co-Director,
Tulane Center for Intellectual Property Law & Culture

New Orleans, Louisiana
February 2011

PHOTOGRAPHS OF THE ERA

Maison Delamare, édit. Yvetot, rep. int.

9. YVETOT (Guerre 1914-15) – Hôpital de " l'Alliance ", fondation Anglo-Américaine – Salle des Isolés

I SAW THEM DIE

To Coco and his friends

EDITOR'S NOTE

WHEN Mrs. Millard placed her diary of 1918 in my hands, I had just finished declaring that in spite of my distaste for violence, I could never quite bring myself to embrace the negative philosophies of pacifism. Today I cannot truthfully repeat this assertion. The part I have played in preparing this manuscript from Mrs. Millard's journal and notes has left its mark on me.

My 1918 was spent in Washington, amid the excitement and glamor of war-time diplomacy. At that distance, war had dignity, nobility, even brilliance. Now that I have seen war through a telescope — I might even say, through a microscope — I can honestly say I have seen enough of it.

Adele Comandini

AUTHOR'S FOREWORD

MY SON Coco is five. It seemed incredible, when I decided to move last October, that in five years one human could have accumulated so many belongings. Coco appears to attract windable and draggable objects as numerously and mysteriously as his youthful companion, Marmaduke II, attracts fleas. But it is not so simple a problem to dispose of them. After going over with my son the question of what might be dispensed with in his elaborate collection of toys, we found ourselves high and dry upon the horns of a dilemma. The things he had used, he'd grown fond of and sentimentally refused to relinquish. Those he had not used, now brought to his attention, were immediately put into action. I had to resign myself to emptying another storeroom trunk of relics, old toys, as it were, of my own, for my son's packing.

Strange that such a trifling domestic adjustment should have propelled me into the preparation of this record. While emptying a dusty trunk I came upon several of my old diaries. One of them I had wrapped in a small French tricolor. It contained my record of the year 1918. After an hour I emerged from the storeroom, the book in my hand, and entered the nursery. Jeannette, our beloved Scotch nana, lifted her eyes from Coco's supper.

"Whatever is the matter, Mrs. Millard?" she asked, the butter-knife poised over a baked potato. "Jeannette," I replied, "I am going to write a book."

S. M.

I

THE DIARY OF 1918 lies before me, a small pigskin volume with a gilt clasp. It is spotted with ink and its binding is broken. I turn the leaves through January and February. They give me a picture of New York during the exciting period when troops were parading down Fifth Avenue and every available church basement, social-hall and "Y" had been converted into a Red Cross center, a relief office or a canteen. The city was seething with men in uniform. Many of the boys I knew had already sailed, and my brothers were at Officers' Training Camps, drilling impatiently against the day they would be ordered overseas.

Our pleasures were keyed to the military pitch. Our beaux and dancing partners came to New York on leave expecting to receive sailing orders at any moment. There was deep mystery about dates and points of departure. Our hearts thumped admiringly to the tune of *Over There.*

Through these pages runs my fierce determination to join the service. The lilt of *Tipperary, Madelon,* and *Roses of Picardy* heated my enthusiasm to fever pitch. I had painful visions of Paris, where I had spent several happy years, overrun by bristle-headed Prussians, clicking their heels and rattling their sabers. I wanted to help save France from the marauding enemy. Banners streamed in my blood. Drums beat in my brain. Bugles sounded in my ears. I wanted to go overseas.

My mother regarded the enthusiasm with tactful indulgence. She told me soothingly that I was far too young and inexperienced to be of any help on the other side. I could do plenty at home, knitting and selling Liberty Bonds. But this was not enough for me. My imagination had caught fire. I visualized myself driving an ambulance along the line of battle, aiding and comforting the wounded, or kneeling beside dying men in shell-torn No Man's Land. Or better still, gliding silently among hospital cots, placing a cool hand on fevered brows, lifting bound heads to moisten pain-parched lips with water. Reading to quiet men with ban-daged eyes. Gently dressing a broken arm or leg. Or bearing the weight of a heroic convalescent as he took his first steps with a crutch.

Perhaps Ted, whom I was then looking upon with some favor, would be brought back to the hospital — wounded. Oh, very slightly wounded, of course. Gassed a bit perhaps. Or with a sprained ankle. He would open his eyes and find me bending over him, my white veil brushing his cheek. He would speak my name, and I would press his hand. Then I would attend him, while his grateful eyes would follow me worshipfully through the ward.

I wanted to go overseas! In spite of refusals, advice and even ridicule on the part of elders and betters, I plagued and persisted. I soon discovered that among the French nurses were badly needed; their long-drawn-out siege of war had depleted the ranks of helpers to an alarming degree. From then on, nothing could stop me. I had two valuable assets — a fair knowledge of French, and the determination that goes with red hair. The diary gives an account of my departure.

March 16, 1918

I am on the steamer with a Volunteer Unit, going to France to help nurse the wounded. So thrilled I can hardly believe it's true. Last night we slept on the deck wrapped in life belts. German submarines sighted, so orders were to sleep near the life boats. The belts are horribly clumsy and uncomfortable, but what of it? C'est la guerre!

Elsie Janis on board. What a personality! Everything is a lark to her. If she can take the war that way, I can too.

Ted was the only one I wanted to see me off at the steamer. He brought me an armful of presents, beside the ones that were delivered to my stateroom. Candy, flowers, books. One of those tiny new wrist watches that I have been dying for. A gold fountain pen to write him with, and of all things, a tremendous patented life preserver that takes up the whole stateroom! I will never hear the end of that from the unit.

T. and I joked about my getting over to France first and he begged me not to win the war until he had a chance at it. In spite of our joking it was hard to say good-by when the moment really came, and the whistles began to blow. We

2

*retired behind one of the boats for our last embrace, think-
ing we were completely hidden from view. I have already
learned that almost everyone on board saw that parting.*

*Now that I am really on the way I have a "gone" feeling. Ted
is gone, home is gone, everything that was safe and sure is
gone. Perhaps I am only hungry!*

*The unit is congenial, but all older than I, and more ex-
perienced. I hardly dare open my mouth for fear they will
find out I am just out of school and have never had hospital
training of any kind.*

It makes me smile now as I remember my anxiety to deceive my
companions. The fact was that very few of them were trained. Like
myself most of them had got through on their enthusiasm and
their exuberant health.

The dismal, dangerous voyage made very little impression upon
me. Exhausted from the excitement of departure, I slept soundly
on the hard deck swathed in my cork nightrobe. During the day, I
read a handbook of nursing in secret, ate chocolate bars, and
counted the final minutes before mealtimes.

Ah, youth! How dauntless thy courage and how insatiable thine
appetite for chocolate bars! I must have eaten at least a hundred
of these on the eight day trip across.

French Red Cross Headquarters, Paris

March 24th

*Landed in Bourdeaux today. Came to Paris immediately
where word awaited us that our unit is to be rushed out to
an emergency hospital near the firing line. It is so exciting
and we are all thrilled to have such luck. Real war at last.
Can hardly wait. Here we go!*

The trip from Paris to the hospital returns vividly to my mind.
Late in the afternoon, after much red tape about getting permission to pass through the boundary into the war zone, they
huddled us into a big covered *camion* with no place to sit down,
but with profuse apologies for the conveyance which had recently

carried a load of mules to the front. It was a lark to us and we crowded in, laughing and clinging together as the clumsy vehicle started. We had been asked to get into our uniforms en route as we would be needed at once upon our arrival. Bouncing along the bumpy roads at breakneck speed, we jokingly repeated *c'est la guerre!* at every bounce, and babbled excitedly over our good luck in getting to the front at once. Lunging from one side of the truck to the other, our suitcases sliding about crazily like dice in a box, we managed somehow to change into the uniforms we had been looking forward with such pride to wearing, and arranged on our heads as best we could without mirrors, the veils of crisp white organdie, with a small red cross embroidered on the forehead, symbols of our coveted importance.

The Hospital was a temporary makeshift, set up hurriedly in a beautiful old château near a part of the line being held by the French and the English against the bitter German offensive. Soissons was only ten miles away. On the lawns surrounding the great stone castle had been erected, almost overnight, rude barracks that held forty or fifty cots each.

Darkness was falling as we arrived. Although, in Paris, we had already heard the boom of guns, our arrival seemed to be the signal for a succession of deafening crashes. We looked at each other. Someone said flippantly: "The fireworks are beginning!" Beginning? The biggest German offensive of the entire war was reaching its climax at this moment, and the allied armies under the new command of General Foch were massed along a fifty-five mile front.

As our *camion* drove through the château gate we could see that the grounds were covered with what looked like sleeping men.

II

French Evacuation Hospital, Château Gabriel

March 24th

As I scribble this we are in the dining hall waiting for coffee before going to work. They offered us food, but we are too excited to eat. However, it is cold and wet, and the coffee will warm us up. A French doctor came in and looked us over hurriedly. He seemed satisfied with what he saw; plenty of health and good nature. Ten American girls waiting for orders. Untrained, perhaps, some of us, but eager to help and ready for whatever comes our way.

March 28th

Terribly busy. It is all so different than I imagined. No time to write.

There was no need to write. The memory remains indelible. Thirty-five hundred cots filled with wounded men. And more pouring in all night from the procession of camouflaged ambulances without headlights crawling slowly along the muddy, shell-rutted roads.

The winter nights were pitch black and much of the way lay through dense woods. To make it more difficult for the ambulances the roads were crowded with troops, supply *camions* and ammunition *caissons;* all without lights . . . crawling through the mud on their way to the front. The grim, black, two-way serpentine seemed endless.

The ambulances could work only during the night for by daylight they would be seen and fired upon by the enemy. No matter at what time of day a man was wounded, he must lie in a second or third line trench dressing station until nightfall. Then the dark caravan began.

Arriving at the château, the men were deposited anywhere on the grounds, on stretchers, waiting their turn to be attended. Although cases that could be moved were evacuated constantly to

5

hospitals farther back, hundreds of wounded men lay out there in the cold and rain, sometimes for three days and three nights, without blankets, before we could make room for them inside. From the black shadows under the trees came their moans, their cries and sobs. Some were unconscious from pain and fatigue.

These were the "sleeping men" we saw when our *camion* arrived. We had to step over them and through them when we were shown to our posts that night. We were distributed about the place where help was most needed and saw almost nothing of each other again for several days.

On the way to my barrack, number 42, at the other end of the grounds and some distance from the château itself, I saw my first airplane disaster. A rocket of red flame cut through the clouds almost directly above, and fell noiselessly through the blackness to blackness beyond. I saw many afterward, but the first had a special significance. It was, like the welcoming barrage and the tramp of marching men on the road below, part of my overture to war.

The door of the barrack was opened cautiously for me to slide quickly through. I went on duty.

Inside, all was confusion, disorder and excitement.

Only dim flickers from candles illumined the chaos. Nurses, doctors, orderlies, beds everywhere; yet not nearly enough to take care of the influx of wounded. That is why they had hurried us through and put us to work at once.

The French hospital system had improved considerably since 1914 and was famed for its efficiency, but it was entirely demoralized during this greatest of all German drives. Hundreds upon hundreds of wounded poured in like a rushing torrent. No matter what we did, how hard we worked, it did not seem to be fast enough or hard enough. More came. It took me several days to steel my emotions against the stabbing cries of pain. The crowded, twisted bodies, the screams and groans, made one think of the old engravings in Dante's *Inferno*. More came, and still more.

Stretcher bearers perspired under their loads until the aisles of every ward were packed. And still the grounds outside were full to overflowing. In the darkness under the trees orderlies stumbled about, giving a hurried drink to parched lips that had cried for water for twenty-four hours. . . . Don't drink too much, pal, we haven't much left, and no time to boil more. . . . Here and there they pulled a blanket over a face. The covered men were carried out quickly to make room for others.

In the ward, orders flew at us. Do this! Do that! We did, as well as we could. No time for explanations or formalities. The preliminary instructions we were to have received from the hospital chief were never given. Our first lesson in nursing was to begin nursing, whether we knew how or not.

Someone thrust a huge hypodermic needle and a packet of some-thing into my hands and told me hurriedly that every man who came in must have a shot against tetanus. The soil of the battlefields was impregnated with poisons from gas and explosives. After that I was to get them ready for the operating table. Hurry! Fast as you can. I looked about helplessly. How on earth did one give a hypodermic? I'd never even *had* one. And what did "get them ready" mean?

I watched another nurse snap the glass tube containing the antitoxin, fill the syringe, and jab the needle in. Taking a deep breath I filled my syringe, shut my eyes, and tried it. Unfor-tunately, my first attempt was on an Arab, and I was horrified to discover that I could not penetrate his flesh with the needle. I called to an orderly and showed him the bent needle; he assured me that it was because Arabs had skin as tough as leather. I attached a fresh needle and tried again. This time it worked. The second, third, fourth times are easier. Soon I am going like light-ning.

But getting them ready is another matter. I watch my colleague closely to see what she does about that. She undresses them, removing all their clothing — boots, leggings, belts, gas-masks, kit bags. She washes their wounds as well as she can with the little tin basin of water and wraps them in a clean sheet to go in to the surgery. The clothes are left in a heap to stumble over in the aisles. I follow her example. It is not easy. My hands tremble as I pull at sodden boots and uniforms. The weather is cold and wet and most of their garments are caked with mud from head to foot, so that to get the things off without causing excruciating pain is almost impossible. "Leave me alone, will you!" they scream wildly and resist my ministrations. Many of them have nothing on their wounds but a strip of coat sleeve or an old muffler or a muddy legging wrapped on quickly by a comrade in the field. Some have only newspaper tied on with a bootlace. I remove blood- and mud-soaked bandages and find an arm hanging by a tendon. *Roses are blooming in Picardy* . . . the silly tune runs inanely through my head. I have a crazy impulse to run. But I stay.

Boom . . . Boom . . . Boom . . . Boom! The big guns roar. The line is only eight miles away. The earth trembles and the flimsy barracks shake with each report. It sounds like a bad thunder storm . . . a hundred bad thunder storms. Flashes from cannon fire light up the cracks around the shuttered windows. I am too busy to be frightened. The blood-soaked clothes and bandages begin to give more easily under my learning fingers.

As I work on one man, bathing the great hip cavity where a leg once was, a long row of others, their eyes fastened upon me, await their turn.

Gashes from bayonets. Flesh torn by shrapnel. Faces half shot away. Eyes seared by gas; one here with no eyes at all. I can see down into the back of his head. Here is a boy with a gray, set face. He is hanging on . . . too far gone to make a sound. His stomach is blown wide open, and only held together by a few bands of sopping gauze which I must pull away. I do so, as gently as I can. The odor is sickening; the gauze is a greenish yellow. Gangrene. He was wounded days ago and has been waiting on the grounds. He will die.

Every now and then the pit of my stomach sinks. I set my teeth and go on. A chest ripped open exposes lungs working feebly and slowing down under my very eyes. I stare fascinated . . . out, in . . . out and in . . . out . . . in . . . weaker and weaker. The next one is already dead; a young blond boy with a questioning look on his face; eyes wide open and cheeks streaked with mud that shows the trace of tears. I pull up the blanket.

My hands get firmer, faster. I can feel the hardness of emergency setting in. Perhaps after a while I won't mind. Here is an unconscious lad with his head completely bandaged. The gauze is stiff with blood and dirt. I cut carefully and remove it, glad he is unconscious; much easier to work when they cannot feel the

8

pain. As the last band comes off, a sickening mass spills out of the wide gash at the side of his skull. Brains! I am stunned. I cannot think what to do. No time to ask questions. Everyone around me is occupied with similar problems. Boldly I wrap my hand in sterile gauze and thrust the slippery mass back as best I can, holding the wound closed while I awkwardly tie a clean bandage around the head. It does not occur to me until afterwards that he must have been dead.

On to the next. He is a short, powerfully built Breton. We used to go to Brittany for the summer . . . to Dinard. He reminds me of Ricou, the porter at the hotel, whom all the children adored. He is groaning with pain and screams deliriously as I begin undressing him. I distinguish in the unfamiliar patois a savage phrase: "I slit him open! Open, I tell you! God damn his soul!" He shakes with sobs. Is it delirium . . . or horror at what he has done?

March 30th

Three days and three nights without a minute's relief. I could go right on, but they sent me up to sleep. Strange, I am not tired. French, British and Canadians poured in last night. And some Americans. I dread to look at them. It brings everything so close. I wonder how soon this will end.

Wounded men in agony coming in . . . coming in . . . coming in, endlessly. Doctors working all day, all night, until they dropped, gulping black coffee and cognac now and then to keep awake, their faces chalk white from exhaustion. I thought Dr. Le Brun really was going to drop that day. He hung onto the door of the operating room and swayed a little. As he stood there I heard him say: *"La gloire, la gloire! Bah! C'est de la merde!"* When he saw me waiting to get past with water and gauze he was embarrassed. *"Pardon, Mademoiselle"* . . . he stepped aside to let me through.

Finally word came that the salient was broken, and the line pushed back two miles. Two miles! My brain went round on the words like a scratched phonograph record. I needed sleep. . . . Two miles of what?

I tossed that night, too tense to get the rest I badly wanted. Two miles. . . . My brain would not let go of the words. Two miles times twenty-two, times two hundred and twenty-two shattered men. How many hospitals does that make? How many men in each hospital? How many dead? How many dying?

"La gloire . . . la gloire" . . . Dr. Le Brun was my favorite of all the surgeons, a brilliant young specialist from Lyons. Good looking, too. I wondered where Ted was . . . his last letter was from Upton. He hoped to be coming over soon. He could hardly wait. I felt years and years older than Ted. I had crossed a river of blood since I had last seen him. How would I feel about him when we met again? At last I slept.

III

April 1st

The big drive is over and the terrific rush has stopped, at least temporarily, but the hospital is still filled.

Most of the men are too badly wounded to be moved, although we need the space, for we are swamped with influenza cases. I thought influenza was a bad cold, something like the grippe, but this is much worse than that. These men run a high temperature, so high that we can't believe it's true, and often take it again to be sure. It is accompanied by vomiting and dysentery. When they die, as about half of them do, they turn a ghastly dark gray and are taken out at once and cremated.

We are better organized now, and able to keep track of pulses and temperatures, and we have some system. There are special wards for the influenza, one for gangrene cases, another one for major gas burns, one for meningitis, one for fractures, one for spinal injuries, and so on. I have worked in all of them and cannot make up my mind which is the worst.

April 3rd

I thought the enemy did not bomb hospitals, but almost every night we are bombarded by German planes. Sometimes thirty and forty overhead at once.

It must be an uncomfortable feeling for the men to lie helpless in bed, with arms strapped up or down, fastened tightly to a frame, or legs in casts, aware that directly over their heads are enemy planes loaded with bombs. The men know the sounds. Boche planes have quite a different motor noise from ours. It is a dismal groan, several tones deeper than the French.

They also seem to know whether the planes are on their way to Paris, and therefore well supplied with bombs of various kinds, gas, incendiary and explosive, or whether they have finished the evening's work and are on the way home. They skip through the air on the home stretch with a jubilant din, instead of the chug-chug of earlier evening.

The only comfort in the whole business is that as soon as one is sighted in the sky, the anti-aircraft guns surrounding the hospital start peppering them from below, and it all creates such a jumble of deafening sounds that we can't tell which are our own noises and which are theirs.

Air raids were a constant and nerve-racking peril. In the middle of one night, during the tense moment in a delicate task, we heard a frightful crash, and the news soon spread that the barrack next but one, filled with wounded men, orderlies and nurses, had been bombed. Save for the ragged remnants of a few who unfortunately survived with further injuries, the ward was gone. Even when I saw it, I could not believe it. My mind refused to accept the fact. I thought the big red cross on the roof made this sacred ground. But it happened again and again.

One night we were bombed for the third time in one week. It was just about dawn. When I rushed out to discover what the explosion had done this time, I saw an unforgettable sight. Against the blood red sky of sunrise stood a tree which had spread its bare branches over one of the barracks. For a moment I could think of nothing but a Christmas tree: the building had disappeared and the barren branches had blossomed horribly with fragments of human bodies, arms and legs, bits of bedding, furniture, and hospital equipment.

April 6th

It has been what they call around here "quiet" for several days now. It is surprising how bored we get with regular hours and plenty of sleep. We work in shifts from four in the afternoon to four in the morning, and vice versa, so that we all get a turn at day and night service.

If anyone had told me I could keep going steadily for twelve hours at a stretch without dropping, I wouldn't have believed it. But now the mere twelve hours seem like nothing after the three-day and three-night grind of last week.

Chapter Three

Took a kodak picture of our quarters the other day to send to the family and it turned out beautifully. It looks like a school dormitory with the ten beds in a row, each bed with a shelf over it for our things. It is easy to see which is mine by the photograph of Ted on my shelf. His picture stands out so clearly you can recognize him. The girls call him Romeo, and I still haven't stopped hearing about our long farewell behind the boat.

Am getting better acquainted with the other nurses and particularly like Suzanne Mercier, a French girl, who helped me through the rush of the first few days by showing me the ropes. She has been here two years. She has a lovely soprano voice and had been training for the concert stage. The men like to hear her sing and she is so nice about it, singing for them whenever they ask her to. She seems to know all their old favorites. I have taught her several American songs and her accent is delightful.

Now we have a chance to look around the château a bit. What a beautiful place it must have been! Today I was surprised to learn that the chatelaine, Madame de Merret, still lives on the place. While I was busy with dressings, I saw the door open and one of the French nurses conducted a small, straight, little old lady in black into the ward. She paused and looked around slowly. Behind her was a very old and wrinkled peasant woman, also in black. Suzanne whispered to me that they were Madame de Merret and her maid. Madame de M. was charming and made it a point to speak to the American nurses who were near at hand, thanking us graciously for our help. The old peasant woman curtsied to each one of us, bending almost to the floor, and blessed us with tears in her eyes. It made us feel rather shaky and choked up. When they went out we felt somehow that a priceless decoration had been pinned right on our bibs.

Having more leisure, I began looking about the château and observed the incongruity of great drawing rooms, billiard and reception rooms, ball rooms and banquet halls, filled with narrow cots. The officers were supposed to be housed in the château, while the soldiers were taken to the barracks; but they were often mixed together in those frantic days before the salient was broken, and officers and men lay side by side in the huge salons of the main edifice, the paneled and damask walls a vivid contrast to the bare practicality of hospital equipment.

The small room used as a pharmacy, where medicines were mixed and dispensed, must have been a dressing room. Here the guests of the chatelaine removed their wraps in the glamorous days before 1914. The room was decorated in pastel colors, with flowers and fat cupids painted in oils upon a gold background. Enormous gilt mirrors covered two walls. In fact, the huge mirrors that hung in all the rooms were sometimes embarrassing. So many things go on in a hospital ward that are best not duplicated and triplicated on every side.

I had several talks with Madame de M. in the weeks that followed and she described to me with restrained fierceness what the Germans had done to her home during their occupancy in 1914. They had used the château for General Headquarters during the days when they had nearly got to Paris. When they were finally driven back, the place was left in ruins. Priceless tapestries in the halls and salons were slashed to ribbons. The delicate inlaid piano in the music room was wrecked and then filled with unused wine from the cellars. Great windows of heaviest plate glass were demolished. Exquisite floors were scarred and marred beyond repair. Trees and rare flowering plants which had taken a hundred and fifty years to perfect had been deliberately destroyed.

Madame de Merret conducted several of us through the grounds and showed us where her tulip beds had been; her English phlox, her fragrant privet hedges. She placed her fragile hand upon the stump of an elm and said in slow, precise English: These were only *my* flowers. My garden . . . that is nothing! But the fine flower of the world . . . those in there, and down there [she looked toward the churchyard], and more to come. . . .

The guns rumbled in the distance. I shall never forget the white despair of her face.

IV

Have been working in the various wards and am rapidly becoming a real nurse. At least there is practically nothing I have not done in the last few weeks.

I have taken care of, individually and collectively, hundreds of French, British, Algerians, Arabs, Zouaves, Senegalese, a number of Americans, and also many Germans.

The Germans are wounded prisoners and on the whole thoroughly unpleasant. Especially the officers, who have been purposely mixed in with the enlisted men to give them a much-needed taste of democracy.

Some of the officers are members of the Kaiser's crack Prussian Guard Division, and bitterly resent the ignominy of capture. They are given the same consideration as our own men and the same care, but they are sulky and arrogant and give orders in a manner that makes our blood boil. We cannot help disliking them. They are the perfect picture of what one imagines an enemy to be. Insolent, cocky and rude. We are actually afraid of them. I always suspect that they may have a hand grenade or some such dangerous weapon hidden under their pillows. I have never trusted any of them since a stretcher bearer was brought in the other night, shot through the leg by a German officer he was helping carry to safety. The Boche badly wounded, could not resist firing one last shot from his stretcher.

I try to imagine how I would feel if I were a wounded prisoner in an enemy hospital. Would I be rude and domineering to the people who were trying to help me? I don't think so. Our own men regard the behavior of the German officers curiously and with contempt.

Today one of them roared at me: "Schwester! Ein trinken wasser!" Somewhat resentful of his tone, I nevertheless began to obey the imperious command. But an English Tommy in a nearby cot raised himself on his elbow and shouted:

"Say please you bloomin' Boche!" The German spat out a venomous answer in his own language. I approached with the glass of water.

"Don't do it, sister," the Tommy pleaded. "Don't give 'im a bloomin' drop till 'e says please. Oh, Gawd," he groaned, "if I only 'ad me two feet so I could up and wring 'is bloody neck." Tommy fell back exhausted. I gave the glowering German his drink of water, and it gratified me to have him utter a sullen "Dankeschöen."

What a job it was to dismantle a German officer and divest him of all his trappings. They carried around literally pounds of brass buttons, buckles, swords, decorations, field glasses, and most of them carried elaborate Leuger automatics inlaid with mother-of-pearl. Almost everything they wore or carried was garnished with black eagles and other weighty insignia. Their voluminous coats had secret pockets and compartments to hold compasses, flashlights, first-aid kits, metal fountain pens and pencils, maps of the sector and other accouterments of a meticulous and mechanized warfare. All this was thrown unceremoniously in a heap outside the ward, to be sorted out later and salvaged with true French thrift. Elegant shining helmets with spiked tops, richly fur-lined gloves and splendidly varnished boots. There were even some beautifully made corsets, real honest-to-goodness corsets, with steels, laces, and all.

April 10th

Had a bath last night. Having a bath in this place is about as private as having one in Times Square. Such a fuss. Never again! Next time I will bathe in a bucket and not breathe a word to a soul about it.

All of us became experts at bathing in a bucket. A pail of hot water and plenty of soap, with a large area to splash around in, became our idea of luxury. A real bath in a tub was such an exhausting performance that it rapidly fell into disuse. The water in the taps was, of course, ice cold. All that was used in the wards had to be heated on top of the rude little coal stoves in the barracks. The regular procedure for a bath went something like this:

I told my orderly that I thought I would take a bath tonight. That meant I would need hot water. He spread the news around among his confreres, and soon there were buckets of water heating on our two stoves, and also on stoves commandeered for the occasion in three or four other barracks. By this time almost everyone knew that Mademoiselle was going to have a bath, and orderlies were rushing back and forth excitedly to report the progress of the water. When it had finally reached the proper degree of warmth, I led the procession up to the nurses' quarters several blocks from the wards, on the topmost floor of the château.

We filed gravely into a vast chamber called a bathroom, filled with elegant marble fittings, none of which seemed to *marche*. It was still as cold as Greenland and a few panes were out of the windows, adding a keen spring gale to the occasion.

My friends, the orderlies, began pouring their buckets of water into the enormous tub with much good-natured discussion and noisy argument as to the comparative merits of doing the thing this way or that way. She should have a sheet in the tub. No, she doesn't want a sheet. Americans bathe without sheets. How droll! Laughter. What about the drain? Is it sufficiently stopped that none of the water will leak out? Yes, it seems quite tight. But Mademoiselle must be careful not to take out the stopper, or she will slide through. More laughter.

The first few buckets made no more impression in the vast tub than if they had been a few glasses. But finally my friends stood off and proudly surveyed the result of their evening's work. About six inches of luke warm water snuggled close to the bottom of the tub. They bowed, smiled and withdrew discreetly.

Next morning all those who had officiated at the ceremony the evening before, rallied 'round and asked politely if Mademoiselle had enjoyed her bath.

You can readily understand why we got into the habit of bathing quietly in a bucket.

April 30th

Am still in the ward with the prisoners. I still dislike the officers but the soldiers, mostly youngsters, are pathetic.

One boy, only sixteen, has visited an uncle in Milwaukee and speaks fair English. He tells me interesting things about the other side of No Man's Land. He is too young to know he should not talk so freely, but we seem to have struck up a little entente cordiale *of our own, and he appears to regard me not as an enemy but rather as a friend, someone he can talk to, particularly about Milwaukee.*

I recall that boy well. He told me earnestly he could not hate America, even though she had entered the war against Germany. He told me he had been very happy with his uncle in Milwaukee, and had intended to return there when he grew up. His eagerness was touching. I'm afraid I made quite a pet of him. I wonder if he ever did get back to America. I doubt it. His right leg was gone above the knee, and his right arm was so shattered he would never use it again. His eyes were large and gentle. His pale, stubby hair was shaved close to his head. A native of one of those simple hamlets in the south, near Oberammergau, he was naïve and well-mannered. He looked gray and under-nourished, and often told me, very confidentially, that he hated the war. At first, he said, it seemed brave and glorious to fight for the Fatherland. But now he did not understand it at all.

Kind *Schwester,* he begged one day, will you have the goodness to write to my mother about me? She will be worried. Tell her I am all right; tell her. . . He did not realize that there was no communication between the two countries at this time. I explained this to him and he was embarrassed. Oh, yes, yes, of course! It was all so strange, difficult for a boy of sixteen to grasp the full significance of bitterness and hatred. Wistfully, he told me about the Christmas box they had sent from home. It contained everything but roller-skates. Of course, his mother could not know what war was really like. She sent him all the things she knew he liked, but nothing that a man could make use of on a field of battle. He described his mother to me and it was obvious that he had never been far from affectionate family ties.

One day while I was doing his dressing he told me something he had heard from a comrade. He told it to me stealthily with pained need for a confidence. It seems, he said, that instead of burying their dead, which was expensive and got them nowhere, a German expert had thought up a new idea for conservation. Thousands of bodies were gathered up, loaded into freight cars and taken to a suburban factory where they were — his voice lowered in horror — they were put into an enormous grinding machine. From the chemically treated remains they extracted some element valuable in the manufacture of high explosives. It sounded lurid, and I assured him that this was merely one of the many myths that circulated about the battlefields. He thought this over in silence. I remembered reading in some book on insect life about a species of warlike ants which used every fragment of their fallen comrades and enemies to fortify their stronghold and feed their warriors. Was it possible, I wondered, that the Germans *had* reached such a point of inhuman efficiency?

Schwester, the boy went on after a thoughtful pause, if I die here, will I be buried?

You are not going to die, I scolded, you are getting well.

But if I should die here, would I be buried? he persisted. I assured him he would. It seemed to satisfy him.

May 10th

Something strange happened in the prisoners' ward today. They are putting all the Germans together as they come in now instead of mixing them in with our own wounded.

While I was undressing a badly injured prisoner, he spoke to me in French, almost in a whisper. He said: "Don't bother undressing me. I'm too far gone. Get me the Agent de Liaison quickly." I was so surprised to hear a German speak such perfect French that I stared at him. He said: "Vite! Je vous en prie. Il n'y a temps à perdre." There was no time to lose, I could see that. There was something about the man's tone and manner that made me run quickly to the study for the Liaison Officer, telling him that one of the German prisoners wanted to see him. He asked: "What does he want?" I did not know. "Does he speak French?" "Yes, very well!" The officer followed me to the ward and when we reached the bedside the wounded man signed to him to bend down. I am still afraid of prisoners and wondered if the man intended to do Major Berthiot some injury. But it seemed to be all right. The Major patted the man gently on the shoulder and said: "Oui, Oui, mon brave, je comprends!" Then he hailed an orderly. Together they wheeled him into the curtained-off

section at the end of the ward, and the head surgeon and his nurse followed them in.

They all stayed in the dressing room with the wounded prisoner for quite a while, over an hour. Then the cart was wheeled out. The man's face was covered. The nurse came out crying, and Berthiot was wiping his glasses. I learned that the man belonged to the French Intelligence, had got into a dead German's uniform and had slipped into the enemy lines. The doctor had kept him alive with saline injections just long enough to get the valuable information he had gathered about the movement of enemy troops. Then he died.

Strange, isn't it, that when a spy is on our side he is a hero, though when he is on the other side he is a detestable sneak.

V

One of the girls just brought up the mail and tossing me a letter, said: "Here's one from Romeo." It was postmarked Brest, but no hint of where he is going from there. It is thrilling to know he is so near but what good will it do? The war will have to last a long time for me to save up enough leave to make it worth while. Let's see — twelve hours every two months. With luck and good management I should be able to take off about three days by the fall.

It is still quiet here, but I have noticed a strange tension in the air and several things have happened that make me realize doctors are definitely human beings. Today as I was coming through the corridor in the officers' ward with a tray in my hands, I met Dr. Girard. I hardly know him; he has been in the theatre, as they call the surgery, almost constantly since I arrived. He stared at me in an odd sort of way and would not let me pass. Then he took the tray from my hands, set it on the window ledge and without further ado, grabbed me in his arms and kissed me vigorously. I struggled free with some difficulty, and he gravely handed me the tray again and began walking along beside me as if nothing had happened, I was quite upset because someone might have come along, but thank goodness no one did. I thought his behavior very undignified and silly and told him so. I tried to hurry away from him but he deliberately kept step with me and although he looked exactly as if we were discussing medical matters, he was calling me all sorts of French pet names and asking me when I would go to Paris with him. I said: "Absolument jamais!" and ducked into a ward. I don't think absolument jamais is very good French but I hope he knew I meant it.

Why doesn't Doctor Le Brun notice me once in a while? Yesterday I saw him in the ward sitting on the bed beside Hansen, a big gawky Swede from Minneapolis who has lost his right arm. Le B. was showing him how easy it is to write with the left hand. Le B. is left handed, does all his op-

erating with his left hand. When he had gone I saw Hansen scribbling away, practicing cheerfully with his tongue tucked out of the corner of his mouth.

If Le B. asked me to go to Paris with him, I'm not so sure I would say Absolument jamais! He is a dear. So good to all the men. Pats them and calls them Mon Petit and Mon Vieux. Not like the cold-blooded, goateed Moreau whom we all dislike, and who works like a mechanical man, without one spark of feeling. One of the surgery nurses told me he began operating the other day before the ether had taken effect.

May 16th

Dr. Le Brun noticed me today. As I was coming out of the surgery with an armful of bottles he smiled at me and said: "Bien fait, bébé, bien fait." Good work, baby, or words to that effect. It may not be exactly an impassioned speech but it is a lot coming from Dr. Le B. He isn't young, must be thirty-five, and he probably has a wife and children — or at least a fiancée down in Lyons. But I hope not.

I seldom have time to think of Ted these days, but when I do get 'round to it, I love him dearly, and perhaps it is best to stick to one's own nationality. I must write to him tonight.

The little contretemps in the corridor with Dr. Girard was only one of the incidents which marked that period of comparative inactivity. Immediately after a big drive, everyone appeared to relax from accumulated fatigue. But after having rested a bit, our heroic doctors would begin looking about them, and it was natural that they should observe and admire the fresh vigor of the American unit. Nearly all of us had some similar adventure to report, and I am bound to confess that some of us were not above flirting outrageously with these not indifferent and altogether interesting males who were naturally somewhat woman-conscious after a long period of grim duty and military segregation. But apart from a normal amount of: "He said and I said . . ." and highly exaggerated accounts of being: "Scared to death, he looked so strange and wouldn't let me go. . ." I think we all emerged from our experiences none the worse, except for an increased opinion of our own seductiveness.

Remembering this period of slightly hysterical romanticism on the part of the hospital staff, I also recall Madame de R., one of the French nurses who had given her services to her country ever since the outbreak of the war. She had become, after the four long years of experience, head surgical assistant to one of the older doctors. She was by no means young herself, but very straight and brisk with hair dyed a reddish gold. She was the only nurse among the fifty odd who used cosmetics; her lipstick and *macquillage* were in the height of Parisian fashion; and her irregular features gave, by some trick of artifice, the impression of extreme attractiveness. I learned that she was a somewhat déclassée *vicomtesse* who had been for years the mistress of the surgeon she assisted. She went with him everywhere as his special nurse. At first we were inclined to resent her privileges and air of authority, but we soon found that she was a grand person, an understanding friend to all of us, and that she genuinely admired our spunk and appreciated our hard work.

Although she had lived a life of mondaine luxury until the war, no one was more efficient and tireless than this nearly middle-aged woman. We learned to love her devotedly. Her iron cot, with a shelf across the head for her belongings on which stood silver-framed photographs of her glamorous intimates, was the Mecca for all who needed a sympathetic ear in which to pour their troubles, real and imaginary.

There were still many details of duty which were not clear in my mind. Knowing she was thoroughly experienced and always glad to give the newcomers a lift, I sometimes went to her for advice. Should I change an uncomfortable dressing for the Canadian Captain without waiting for the doctor's orders? Could I ask an orderly to help me feed the bad cases so their food would not get cold? Was it all right to give an extra dose of morphine where the first had not given enough relief? She was so understanding and practical and never failed to make the humane decision which, during the first days, I hesitated to make for myself.

I recall the occasion of my first visit. She was propped up on her cot, against elaborately embroidered pillows, a fine lace boudoir cap on her red locks, wearing a sacque with lace frills at the throat and wrists. A rich silk comforter was thrown over the bed and her beautiful linen sheets were marked with a coronet and a monogram. I felt like a country mouse in my blue flannel dressing gown and knitted slippers, and sat quite awe-struck on the edge of the bed feeling as though I were having an intimate audience with the queen. In her relaxed moments Madame de R. was every inch the Parisian *vicomtesse,* and her splendor was a striking contrast to the gray bathrobes and drab army blankets on the other cots in the room.

May 17th

Machine Gunner Hansen is demoralizing the ward. Now that he is in a wheel chair and can get around, he scoots all over the place teaching the French boys to shoot dice, and I must say they take to it like ducks to water. He uses the board Le B. has rigged up on his chair for writing-lessons, as a dice table. His pupils call him **Professeur,** *and don't seem to mind that he wins most of the time, and comes out two or three suppers ahead nearly every evening. Their belongings being kept in a safe box at the end of each ward, all the men have to gamble with is their trays. Sometimes I hear them say as they roll the dice: "My soup against your coffee. How about it?"*

May 18th

Took a long walk with Dr. Le Brun today. The woods were beautiful and I will never forget that walk. If I thought he was wonderful yesterday, I think he is much more so today. We talked and talked about so many things — partly in French and partly in English. He is shy about speaking English, although he really does very well. We fill in here and there with whichever word fits best and have a grand time. He has a delightful sense of humor. I discovered that today, and it is a dangerous thing to find out about someone you already like a lot. As we strolled along he surprised me by stopping suddenly and saying: "Ah, bon jour, Moreau!" I turned in dismay, expecting to greet the unpopular Dr. Moreau, but all I saw was a scraggy old goat, moving his chin whiskers up and down as he munched from the bushes. The resemblance was so ludicrous and my relief so intense that I laughed until I was weak.

Le B. asked me if I had ever been in love. I said: "No." I don't feel tonight as if I ever **have** *been really in love. I wonder if Ted would mind if I shifted to somebody else, especially a*

Frenchman. *I wouldn't be surprised if I completely forgot Ted, that is if Le B. shows any further signs of interest.*

As we walked along, the roads were like bee-hives, with French troops moving forward although at the moment we are not very near the line. We had to step to the side to let them pass. Hundreds of poilus, *singing* Madelon *as they swung along, their gray-blue overcoats pinned back at the knees.*

Then a regiment of Americans, some marching, some in trucks and others astride the guns on the great cumbersome tractors. They were all grinning like pleased youngsters on the way to a picnic. One of them leaned down and shouted: "Hey, listen, where is all this trouble anyway?" That sticks in my mind for some odd reason. It seems to be the spirit of the entire A.E.F. They don't know what they are in for, and I do. Yet I am glad to see them marching up to the front. How can I be glad? It is all very puzzling. It must be because everything is so topsy-turvy these days.

Le B. remarked as they passed that one could see the difference in temperament between the French poilu *and the American doughboy by the way they wear their helmets. The French plant theirs solidly on their heads, having learned from bitter experience that this is where they will do the most good. But our boys still wear theirs cocked jauntily over one ear.*

Then Le B. and I had quite a heated argument as to whether it is better to be serious about life, or to take it all as a joke; but that didn't get us very far because we both had to agree that you are born one way or the other and that is the way you stay, whether you like it or not.

We found the most beautiful carpet of lilies of the valley growing wild under the trees. The stems grow eighteen inches high and the blossoms are enormous. A great bunch of them are beside me in my toothbrush glass as I scribble this and the fragrance is overpowering. We picked armfuls of the lovely things and on the way home stopped in the churchyard and put a few on some of the graves. With a few in my belt and a spray in his buttonhole, we strolled back through the high-walled lanes to supper, the inevitable prime ribs of horse, au jus.

My admiration for Le B. increased daily, although he gave no sign of anything but the most impersonal interest in me. We took many more walks together and the rest of the unit teased me about Le B. and would not believe that our friendship remained on a purely spiritual plane. When he went to Paris on leave he did not, like the impetuous Dr. Girard, ask me to go with him, and in his absence I missed him far more than I would have cared to admit. However, he paid me the compliment of leaving his treasured Belgian police dog in my care. It was the first time he had ever been separated from his dog and the bereft animal wandered about the wards looking for Le B. with a tragic look in his eyes. When someone petted him, he appeared not to see them at all, but looked right past them and merely tolerated the caress. Then, hoping perhaps that his idol was closeted in the surgery, as he so often was for hours and hours at a time, the dog would take his place beside the surgery door, his magnificent head on his paws, and look up alertly at everyone who went in or out. I do not know which of us missed Le B. more, but apparently he did, for the doctor's absence did not interfere with my healthy appetite, whereas I could scarcely persuade the dog to eat a mouthful until Le B. returned.

May 20th

Dr. Le B. is back and Sergeant is happy once more. I thought the dog would go wild when he came in, and I must admit my own heart did a nip-up.

This afternoon he brought a good-looking young French officer into my ward and introduced him to me. He is a lieutenant in the Alpine Chasseurs, the famous Blue Devils. I don't think I have ever seen such a handsome man. He is encamped near here with his regiment, en repos. He is tall, with black hair and very white teeth . . . to say nothing of dark flashing eyes. He wears his beret on the side of his head with rakish swanky. His name is René Gascard. He spoke a little English, and made the most amusing faces trying to remember the right words upon being introduced. When he finally got them out, his eyebrows went up and he gave a dazzling grin as he said proudly: "I spik good ze Hinglish, non?" I said: "Non!" and he laughed and laughed.

He went through the ward with me as I made rounds, pushing the dressing cart along jauntily with one hand as though it were a baby carriage, greeting the men with such good spirits that he left a wake of buoyancy behind him. As I stopped to take temperatures and mark the charts, he stood at the foot of the beds, each in turn, his feet planted sturdily apart, his thumbs hooked in his belt, asking kindly questions and distributing his cigarettes through the ward as jar as they would go. His interest was genuine and there was no trace of the usual condescension between officer and men. I hope we will see more of him.

René came in several times to see Le Brun, and one afternoon I made tea for them in the little curtained-off cubbyhole at the end of the barrack that was used for big dressings which could not be done in the cots. We used a Sterno lamp and a German helmet to brew the tea in, and Le B. ran up to his quarters for saccharine, which we had to use instead of sugar. I contributed chocolate bars from my apparently inexhaustible supply. I think thousands of them were given to me when I sailed and more had been sent from home. The question of cups arose but we soon settled that by drinking our tea with relish out of *ventouse* cups. They are glass suction cups that were used in pneumonia cases.

René was in love with a girl in Dijon and they were going to be married as soon as the war was over. He showed us a miniature of her which he carried romantically over his heart, and when he spoke of her his handsome face became radiant. He was not in the least ashamed of showing his emotions regarding her, and it was arranged right there over the *ventouse* cups that L. was to be best man at the wedding.

We had a pleasant half hour behind the dressing room curtains, and then I had to bundle them off and return to pulses, temperatures and hypos.

May 23rd

I like Dr. Clément. He met Liz and me in the village today and bought us hot chocolate in the bistro. It was vile stuff, made with water, but he made a great joke of it and de-

clared it was made of milk from the sacred bull of some-thing or other. He is awfully amusing, a hale and hearty type. He showed us a snapshot he was sending to his wife of himself with his arms around three of the American nurses and had written on the back: Avec mes petites harlots. *I am beginning to get accustomed to the French sense of humor.*

Saw Madame de R. coming out of the fruiters' with her doctor. He was loaded with packages. She never goes into the village without bringing back a supply of oranges, choc-olates and special treats for the men in her ward.

May 27th

Bad news. The **Boches** *have captured* **Chemin des Dames.** *That gives them a vital strategic position and control of an important approach. It seems to mean a lot because everyone is in the dumps and going about with worried faces. The study is a madhouse and I have never heard French spoken so rapidly or so tensely.*

Their big hope seems to be the Americans who are fighting at Cantigny. I have never been much good at praying, but I am praying now with all my might.

May 28th

The Americans have taken Cantigny. **Vive les Americains!** *My, but we are proud of them!* **Suzanne Mercier sang Yankee Doodle** *all day and the French* **poilus** *joined in.*

A member of the Lafayette Escadrille came in today, a grand-looking ace, with one of his legs smashed. He doesn't seem to mind. Thinks he's lucky to have got off with his life. The leg will probably have to come off but he doesn't know it yet.

His plane crashed after he had brought down two enemy bombers. Major Berthiot came to see him and made a terrific fuss.

The American flyer was awarded a *Croix de Guerre,* and the Hospital Chief was notified that the decoration would be dropped upon the hospital grounds by his flying mate at a certain hour of a certain day. At the appointed hour we heard the roar of a plane flying very low. Our flyer was in the surgery having his leg amputated, and I was holding his hand. He had refused anything but a local anesthetic and wanted to wait until after the ceremony, but the leg was infected and had to come off without further delay. Le B. performed the amputation. I ran to the window and watched the plane maneuver and gave them a full description of what was happening.

There was a group of officials on the grounds as the plane circled twice, then once again above the hospital. The roar became deafening as he came down lower and lower. I grew very excited and cried: "He's flying terribly low. Goodness, it looks as if he's going to come right down on their heads!" Our patient laughed: "That's Dodie," he said, "he's a flying jack-ass." I went on: "He's leaning out! He's dropping a package! He leaned right out and dropped it and Major Gorot caught it. There he goes, swooping back up, waving his hand. They're all waving and cheering at him."

I watched the plane climb back into the blue and then returned to my patient. His eyes were shining, and I am sure he hardly noticed what was being done to him. The only thing that was on his mind was whether he'd be able to fly with an artificial leg. I am certain he was in pain in spite of the anesthetic, for there was a white line around his mouth as he talked and grinned. When it was over he gave a sob and fainted.

He regained consciousness in the ward. I was still holding his hand, and several of the hospital officials were standing around his bed. He looked ghastly, with every ounce of color gone from his face. Opening his eyes, he stared around and then gave me a sheepish grin and hung onto my hand as though begging me for moral support. I gave him a drink of water and then the liaison officer, Major Berthiot, presented the decoration in the name of the French Government and pinned the medal on his breast, going through the usual procedure of kissing the hero on both cheeks. This made him blush to the roots of his hair, so that he looked quite normal again, and he thanked the officer in the worst French I have ever heard, though it was made picturesque by his rich Kentucky drawl.

I believe his name was Dixon and he came from Louisville.

June 1st

Suzanne Mercier dropped in to say good-by to me. She has volunteered to go out with a field unit, one of the traveling hospitals that goes as close to the front line as possible.

Wish I'd known about it. I would have liked to go along.

Letter from Ted. He is at an Artillery School. Hopes to get into action soon. Wonders what it's like. I hope he never finds out.

VI

Poor Suzanne Mercier. We will never hear her singing in the wards again. The ambulance unit was bombed and Suzanne was killed. Also two of the orderlies.

Le Brun broke the news to me and I am sick about it. I liked her best of all the younger French nurses. She was so gay and charming.

The field unit had gone to Pierrefonds, just behind the front line, to station themselves at the château there, which is said to have belonged to Porthos, one of the Three Musketeers of Dumas. The unit consisted of ten *camions,* all with large red crosses painted on top of them. One was a compact surgery, one was for dressings, another for doctors' quarters, another for nurses, and so forth.

They had established themselves close by the château and were just getting into action when they were bombed. Three of the *camions* were completely demolished, all their equipment smashed or scattered. They had to scramble back to the hospital as best they could.

The entire hospital was saddened by Suzanne's death, and my sense of personal loss was intense.

June 3rd

We have a colorful character in one of the wards, badly wounded. He is young, not more than twenty-two, and really a likeable youngster. Always polite and considerate. His name is Pierre Du Clos. Today when I took his temperature, he asked me how it was. I answered, "Quite good" although it wasn't good at all. He gave me a grin and said: "I'm a tough one, Mademoiselle. I'll pull through all right. Only the good die young." Then he asked me if he could have a cigarette. I lit one for him. After all, the poor boy may as well have whatever gives him a bit of pleasure. I doubt if he will last more than a few days. Bad internal injuries.

As I attended a corporal several cots away from Pierre, he asked about Du Clos' condition. I replied that he had a good chance. I don't like to depress the men with discouraging news.

"Do you know who he is, Mademoiselle?" the corporal asked. I said, "No," and got quite a shock when he said: "That boy is one of the toughest underworld characters in Paris. He is the killer for a big Marseilles gang. He had plenty of notches on his knife before he got to the battlefield. If he pulls through this war, he'll end up on the guillotine." I could not believe it and asked my talkative patient how he knew this. He replied that Pierre was in his company and often bragged about his connection with the underworld.

"He's a soft talker," said the corporal, "but plenty tough in action. He comes from Senlis, not far from here."

I can hardly believe that slim, blond boy is an underworld character, and yet I must admit there is something furtive about his eyes, and his chin is ugly. Perhaps I only imagine this because I have heard such a lurid tale about him. But after all, one cannot discriminate between killers at a time like this. It's being done nowadays, by the best people.

As I was leaving the ward, Pierre beckoned to me and asked me a favor. He expected some visitors, and when they came he wanted me to tell them he was on the mend but could not be disturbed. He didn't want to see anyone until he got well. Apparently, his helplessness rankled and he preferred not to be seen at a disadvantage. There was something valiant about the boy's pride. I could not help respecting it, and passed word on to the nurse who relieved me.

June 6th

A slight lull while the line is being held at Montdidier. Just held, no more. Our wards are full, but instead of the steady stream coming in all night, we have only an occasional batch from some small engagement. They are fortunate because now they can have more careful attention than during a rush.

One of the American Ambulance drivers brought me a little red fox last night from Belleau Wood. It cannot be more than a few weeks old and looks like a police puppy. Haven't named it yet. I would have named it after the boy who gave it to me, but I don't know his name. Although he comes in here with his ambulance almost every night and I really know him well, we have never bothered about names.

I was given a dressing cart of my own today. It looks like a tea wagon, but in place of sugar and little cakes, there are iodine and alcohol, probes and cotton, bandages, and so on. I wheel it up beside the bed when I have a dressing to do, or one to change, and if it is a difficult one, the orderly helps me, and hands me instruments and gauze. It is his job to keep it supplied at all times as I am supposed to be too busy to attend to such details. Makes me feel quite important.

Tonight I will be in charge of a ward alone for the first time, so must get some sleep.

That night was memorable. It was raining torrents, a summer downpour. The place leaked like a sieve, and buckets had to be replaced constantly. There were about forty wounded men in the ward, and I had a four-page list of orders to carry out. A candle flickering in a bottle was the only light I had to work by. First I inspected all the charts, as I had not been in this ward for several days and there were some cases I had never seen before. Pierre Du Clos was still there. His chart read: "Internal hemorrhage. Sinking. Watch." I could see he was going fast. I stood by his bed wishing I could do something for him. He looked so young. The toughness was gone. His face was as white as the pillow he lay on. As I watched him, he opened his eyes and looked up at me. His look was deep with terror. He tried to sit up, but I put him back gently, soothing him as best I could. He seized my hand and gripped it until it hurt. His breath was coming in gasps and his pallor became more intense. "Don't let me die," he whispered thickly. "Please don't let me die. Do something . . . give me something. I don't want to die!" He looked up at me desperately, hanging onto my hand in his panic. But there was nothing I could do. I had to let him die, and his hand gradually loosened its hold. Three a.m. I was absolutely alone. There was no one to call as there usually was. Could I have done something, I wondered? Could I have saved him?

A kindly sergeant across the aisle, who had been awake and watching, reminded me to put a screen around the bed until an orderly came to take him out.

Voices drifted through the ward: Nurse! . . . A drink of water! . . . Morphine! . . . My cast is rubbing! . . . My bandage has slipped. . . . Here and there a groan of pain.

I set up the screen and went about my tasks, but my hand shook the rest of the night and I spilled medicines and botched hypos. Pierre's childish terror of death had unnerved me.

Two days later I was in the same ward. The door opened and a little old French couple came in timidly. The man had a stiff bouquet of flowers in his hand, spring flowers from a country garden. The woman carried a covered basket with spotless napery showing at the corners. They scanned the beds eagerly as they came up the narrow aisle toward me, smiling and confident. I went to them and suddenly realized who it was they were asking to see: their son, Pierre Du Clos. Someone in his regiment had told them Pierre was in this hospital, and at the office his death was evidently not yet recorded, so they had been sent to the ward. I had to tell them he was no longer here. . . . I did the best I could to break it gently, but I shall never forget their faces, changing from hopeful anticipation to ghastly understanding. They clung together comforting each other and asking me pitiful questions. Did he suffer much? Did he ask for Papa and Maman? Was he brave? I answered what I thought would give them the most comfort and we all cried together. Their innocent grief was heart-breaking. I led them out to the little churchyard beside the chapel where Pierre was buried with the rest of the heroes. The grave was new; there was still fresh soil on it, and it was marked only by a bit of paper stuck on a stick. I assured them he would have a cross like the rest with his name and his regiment inscribed on it, and the little blue, white and red rosette that each grave bore. They were very plucky and looked about them as though they felt they had no right to grieve for one when there were so many.

I promised to take a snapshot of the grave when it was completed and send it to them. They were pathetically grateful for this and through their tears they told me they were proud to have given a son to France. Pierre had been a good boy. He had a fine position in Paris and had provided for them generously. They could never thank me enough for my kindness to him. The mother lifted the lid of the basket to show me all the nice things she had brought for Pierre: a roast chicken, fresh butter she had made, and everything he liked. Wouldn't I please take it? I could not refuse their simple kindness, and later distributed the delicacies in the ward — in memory of Pierre Du Clos, cutthroat and hero.

I took the picture of Pierre's grave when it had been properly completed, and saw to it that the spot was well covered with flowers before I snapped it. The beautiful letter I received from the two old people brought on another flood of tears. I was glad they never knew what the corporal had told me.

June 10th

I am growing very fond of Bouillotte. *That's what the men have named my little pet fox. It means hot-water bottle. They call it that because it loves to crawl down under the covers of the beds and sleep against their feet. They are all devoted to it and take turns at having it in their beds. So far* Bouillotte *is as gentle as a kitten, but they tell me that I will have to let it go before long, as they say it will get mean and wild. I hate to think of parting with it, for it seems to know me and trots after me to be fed. It is fed constantly with odds and ends from all the trays and acts as if the food is exactly what it has always been accustomed to.*

I have finally had to put a tiny bell on its neck in order to know where it is, as none of the men will admit Bouillotte *is in his bed for fear I will take it away. But now I go around and shake the foot of their beds and when I hear the bell, there is* Bouillotte.

June 12th

Marechal Joffre visited the hospital today. Bouillotte *disgraced me, the little beast. I should get rid of him.*

General Joffre's visit did more to cheer up the wounded men than anything I had seen. He was a dear little old man, short and rosy, and when I saw him I understood why they called him Papa Joffre. The fatherly way he greeted all the men, beaming on them with genuine pride, shaking hands here and there, placing a kindly hand on their shoulders, kissing on both cheeks those few who had the *Médaille Militaire* pinned on their pillows, made one think of him as an affectionate parent rather than a military commander.

Bouillotte gave me a bad quarter of an hour on this great occasion, and the only thing I can say for his behavior is that he sent a ripple of laughter through the ward, and laughs were rare in those days.

As Joffre came in the door, several officials who had accompanied him, and all our highest ranking doctors, liaison officers, and the like, were lined up saluting him stiffly. Their buttons were polished for the occasion, their uniforms newly pressed, and it was all extremely formal and correct. We stood at attention, and those men who could, raised themselves a bit and saluted the General.

Suddenly the little fox, who was strictly an *ex-officio* member of the hospital staff, decided to join the reception committee. He squirmed out from under the covers at the foot of one of the beds and before anyone could stop him he had trotted through the aisle, jingling his bell and dragging his dirty, well-chewed string behind him. He went straight up to Papa Joffre and began sniffing inquisitively at his boots and breeches, as I rushed forward, mumbling a guilty apology, and with some difficulty managed to capture my impudent protegé while the officers and doctors surrounding the general relaxed and laughed. The entire ward joined in the laughter. *Bouillotte* had evidently broken the ice of formality, for when I returned after locking my pet in a supply closet, I found Papa Joffre genially making the rounds.

In spite of his bad behavior I kept *Bouillotte* another month. Then he began to grow too large for coddling, and there was also the possibility that he might revert to type and become savage. So with some reluctance I gave him to one of the ambulance drivers to take back to Belleau Wood where he had come from.

I have often wondered how poor little *Bouillotte* felt to be turned loose in the dark thundering wood after his life of ease at the hospital, and his meeting with the General. I wonder what he told the other foxes about his friendly experience with the age-old enemy who had always hunted his kind to death with dogs and horses.

Some years later I met General Joffre at a dinner in Washington, and I reminded him of the incident of our first meeting. He declared he remembered it very well and gave such an amusing account of *Bouillotte*'s behavior that we all had a grand laugh. The little red fox was still good for breaking ice.

VII

June 14th

We have had a baby.

At least, that is the way everybody feels about it, although it was really Emilie, a little kitchen helper who had it, to everyone's amazement — including her own.

Last night one of the orderlies, Lucien, came rushing into my barrack all excited and wanted to know if Dr. Clément was there. He was not, and I learned from the agitated Lucien that there were great goings on in the domestics' tent. Not wanting to miss anything, I ran out there and found that a little peasant girl we have seen about now and then, as she peeled potatoes under the trees, and whom they called Emilie, was about to have a baby. From what I could gather in the jabbering crowd that had assembled about the poor youngster's cot, the event had come as a surprise to her, although she had been more or less suspicious for some days that all was not as before. Her condition had become apparent, but no one knew when to expect the worst.

Dr. Clément was hastily summoned and we were surprised to learn that in civilian life, before the war, he was a great baby specialist in Paris. And there, amid all that chaos and disorder, with the guns booming faintly but with unfailing regularity in the distance, a son was born to Emilie, whose last name nobody seems to know and about which Emilie herself is a bit doubtful. She has no family, no connections of any kind. As to the paternity of the baby, about that she is also vague. But it was brought into the world by a great specialist, and Emilie loves it and thanks the good God for it since she will now no longer be alone in the world.

It is all very touching and everyone is excited and thrilled over the simple event of Emilie's war baby.

I remember how kind Dr. Clément was to the bewildered girl; he took care of the nameless infant with as much interest as if it had been an heir of royal blood. It thrived under his expert supervision and, somewhat to his consternation, Emilie eventually named it Clément after him. I doubt if many more fortunately born babies have ever had more nurses or more attention than Dr. Clément's namesake. We used to spend all our spare moments holding the baby and walking about with it, making the excuse that it needed fresh air, which it most certainly did. Its bed was a canned milk box beside Emilie's cot in the servants' tent, along with some thirty or forty others, and you may be sure that the dreaded night air was never allowed to penetrate into it.

Emilie bloomed under the sudden rush of attention, and assumed the role of local madonna with complacency. Being wholly unprepared for the event, she had neglected to provide a layette for her child. But soon garments of strange and mysterious origin began pouring in upon the infant, until it was amply if not appropriately clothed. Sets of long gray underwear that had obviously shrunk so that the donor could no longer get into them; an extra tunic that one of the tender-hearted orderlies could manage to do without; bits of feminine lingerie converted into little sacks and petticoats; even a good wool blanket that one of the rheumatic cooks could ill afford to spare. These and other touching tokens bore witness to the tolerant democracy of war.

Madame de R. appointed herself chief godmother to the new arrival and whenever anything new was needed for him she managed to see to it, with her usual efficiency, that the item was produced as rapidly and unaccountably as a rabbit out of a hat.

June 16th

Walked into the village today and while the others were doing errands, I slipped away and had the funny little barber cut off my hair. He has been to the war and hops about on one leg with a crutch.

When I explained what I wanted, he refused point blank to do the dastardly deed. Cut off such beautiful hair? Non, non, jamais! When I insisted that it was only a nuisance, he wrung his hands, raised them to the skies, dropped them in despair and nearly had hysterics. Why, why did I want to do such a dreadful thing? Men do not like masculine girls! Excusez moi, Mademoiselle, but you will certainly regret it. I ignored his pleas and told him firmly to cut it first to the shoulders, so, and then I would tell him what to do next.

Finally he sharpened his shears, and still protesting, he whacked it off with as much finesse as one would use to dock old Dobbin's tail.

It is all bristles and, without a doubt, hideous. I'm afraid I don't look at all like Irene Castle.

June 17th

Today Admiral Plunkett was brought into my barrack. Great excitement to have an American admiral in France and especially in this sector. They marvel at his simplicity and lack of pomp. He has been sent here to recover from a bad cold and all he wants is peace and quiet; but they feel that they must make a fuss over him while he is here. He tells me to say he is asleep whenever he hears footsteps approaching that might mean a formal visit from some dignitary or stiff neck *as he calls them.*

It seems he is in this vicinity setting up a new long-range gun he has invented or perfected, or something.

He says he hopes it will break up some of those kaffee klatches *in Berlin.*

I joked with him about his ragged collection of decorations with ribbons all faded and frayed, and offered to renovate them for him. There is a small shop in the village where they sell medals, decorations, and insignia. I was able to match all the ribbons and sewed them on the medals. The Admiral is resplendent once more and greatly pleased. He says he has had some of the decorations for twenty years and no one ever thought of rejuvenating them before.

I showed him my short hair and he likes it because he says it is so sensible. He says that all women will be cutting off their hair one of these days. I doubt that, but he is an old dear and we are becoming fast friends.

June 20th

Volunteers wanted for another field unit and I am going. I hear Dr. Le B. is to be one of us, though why they would let him go is more than I can understand.

I have made my will. Each one of the girls has told me what she would like to remember me by: Mary, the rest of the chocolate; Liz, my hot water bottle; Janey, my steamer rug. The rest all said: "I'll take Romeo!" But the picture of Ted in the silver frame goes with me. They are going to be quite disappointed when I come back!

I recall that strange journey. We were five nurses, several doctors, and about six orderlies. We started at nightfall for a position immediately behind the firing line, a distance which, under ordinary circumstances, we could easily have covered in an hour. However, without lights and with the roads so badly rutted by gun tracks and shell holes, we took almost three times that long. As we crawled along I noticed a peculiar tapping sound on the roof and sides of our *camion,* a sound like heavy hail, and I learned that it was a rain of bullets from our own anti-aircraft guns falling from the skies. . . . Tap, tap, tap, tap, tap, tap. . . .

The *camions* went very close to the line and we were frantically busy. A continual stream of wounded were brought from the trenches, about four miles away, without even stopping at the dressing stations and the crude wounds were shocking. Many of the casualties were American Marines. We were in a fiercely disputed area and moved back and forth as the line shifted. There was very little time to think of our own danger and we appeared to be providentially spared, for although bombs fell all around us, we did not have a recurrence of the disaster at Pierrefonds.

However, one of our doctors, who had ventured close to the line with an ambulance, returned with a gruesome report that gave us all the horrors. He was talking to one of the officers at the entrance of a rear line dug-out when suddenly there was the whistle of a shell and the doctor's companion was headless. Decapitated before his very eyes. The blood from the officer's jugular vein spurted into the doctor's face and before the headless body fell to the ground it took a few staggering steps, its arms moving jerkily.

This was only one of the grisly happenings of our sojourn behind the front line. One afternoon, toward dark, we had just finished loading an ambulance with wounded whom we had carefully bandaged and made as comfortable as possible for their night's journey over the rough roads to the nearest base hospital. The ambulance driver hopped into his seat and started the motor, calling out a cheery: "A bientôt!" François, one of our favorite orderlies, ran along beside the conveyance and swung himself on board. The ambulance started slowly over the rutted fields to the road beyond. It was still light enough for us to see it turn into the road, and then there was a loud explosion. We saw our newly loaded ambulance peppering the evening sky with flying fragments. The car must have exploded a dud that was lying in the road, and there was hardly enough left of any of them, François, ambulance driver, or *blessés,* to be identified.

This was so close that I could not help thinking the girls might get my belongings after all. I now recall that my friend, Dr. Le B., was not sent with us; the unpopular Moreau was in charge of the *camions.* He had a nasty experience and I couldn't help being pleased that it had happened to him rather than to someone I liked.

One day he returned with a loaded ambulance, leapt to the ground, and quickly divesting himself of his uniform, boots and all, he walked to the doctors' *camion* in his long gray wool underwear and looked very funny doing it as he was rather plump around the middle.

I then saw an orderly come out and pick up the clothes on the point of a bayonet and carry them to the trash fire. I learned later that while M. had been making rounds behind the line he had accidentally stepped into a muddy ditch. His foot sank through the mud into something firm, but yielding, and before he could withdraw his weight there was a loud report like a shot. The explosion had come from the ditch and had covered M. with mud mixed with the unmistakable odor of a decayed cadaver. He had evidently stepped on the swollen stomach of a body that had sunk out of sight in the mud and the noxious gases of decay had exploded under the weight of his foot. In telling the story, the orderly said: "It must have been a *Boche, mam'selle.* No Frenchman could ever smell so bad."

The high and mighty Moreau had to borrow a corporal's uniform for the rest of our stay.

June 26th

Back to the château. It is like home to us. I am beginning to feel that I have always lived here, like this. The years before the war seem long ago, unreal and indistinct.

We have a regular meal at midnight, provided we have time to go and get it. Stale bread, sour wine and lentils or plain macaroni. It is all laid out on the long table and it tastes good too.

I could not help thinking tonight at supper of only a few months ago at home. Supper at midnight . . . in the Crystal Room of the Ritz.

Lobster timbales, *white wine and an ice smothered in* marrons glacés.

Our escorts, smart young officers just out of Plattsburg. Their chief concerns in life were where they had their boots made, the polish they preferred on them, the cut of their uniforms and the angle of their caps. Who saluted whom first, according to their newly acquired rank, was of the gravest importance. We were nearly as much impressed with them as they were with themselves.

Clasped tightly to a Sam Browne belt we danced till dawn to the moving strains of There's a Long, Long Trail Awinding *and nearly burst with emotion.*

We talked wisely about the war. It might as well have been the hereafter for all any of us knew about it.

VIII

July 13th

No letter from Ted. I wonder where he is.

July 15th

There is great excitement in the study where the movements of the armies are followed like a game of chess, with little flags on a map. Bulletins come in hourly by telephone from the front. They say there will be another big German offensive at Soissons only about ten miles from here, and American regiments are being sent up to the line.

The hospital is being evacuated as quickly as possible and put in readiness for another rush. I dread it.

The line is zig-zagging toward us one day and receding the next, and there has been much firing and roaring of guns for the past few nights.

We are cautioned to be particularly careful about lights, and it is a serious offense for even an officer to use a cigarette lighter outside. Once in a while someone stands in the entrance of a barrack holding the door open for a moment, but he is soon reminded that this is not a popular practice by the boos and yells of: "Idiot!" and "Fermez la porte!" from the men inside. Dr. Le B. is back from a quick visit to Paris. No time for walks or talks. Everyone terribly jumpy. The doctors spend all their spare time in the study moving the flags and discussing the movement of the line.

The suspense of those days! At any moment the shelter over our heads might be shattered by shells. The roar of planes above and the rat-tat-tat-tat of *mitrailleuse* was a constant obbligato to the ward routine.

The sound of singing, marching men came from the road beyond. The song they sang at the top of their lungs was *Mademoiselle from Armentières, Polly Voo. . . .* I could see them in my mind's eye, jaunty and fresh, their guns on their shoulders, their helmets cocked over one ear. . . . "Hey, listen, where is all this trouble anyway?"

Inside, the hospital was electric with a rigid silence. The hundreds of empty cots appeared to be waiting, resting. We knew they would soon be filled again — perhaps by morning. Everyone seemed to be waiting; unconsciously we talked in whispers.

And then it came.

July 28th

Have not written for nearly two weeks. Today when I came up to our room to change my uniform, much soiled after working fourteen hours in the wards, I looked down from the big windows and could see the grounds — once more a sea of stretchers, a human carpet.

So many Americans. I hate to see them pouring in, yet I am proud of them. Such gallantry, such nerve, such pluck! Even the French nurses have remarked about it. Always: Thank you, for every little thing. And: How soon will I be able to go back to the line? And: Help him first, he has waited longer than I have.

I feel they are mine, every last one of them, and their downright grit makes me want to cry all over them. Now I know what real nobility means.

Am too sympathetic to make a good nurse. I want to explain to each man all about his wounds and reassure him, and tell him how fine the doctors are and that they will fix him up as good as new.

They seldom know what is the matter with them, but only that they are about to go under an anesthetic and that something is going to be done to them. Can't help thinking that if I were going to be operated on it would be an awfully important event and I would most certainly like to know something about it. So I try to tell them what the doctor will probably do, though more than half the time I don't know myself and I just make up something that sounds plausible and reassuring. They seem grateful and go into the surgery a little less bewildered.

Our efficient detachment of mind was shaken in those days. We were no longer compassionate sympathizers but active combatants. The war had come home to us.

Again the old excitement; the rush, the noise of guns and trembling of the earth from exploding shells. But this time it was different. This time the guns shook our blood; the shells exploded in our very hearts.

Here was a boy from Nebraska. I began unwrapping some sodden leggings from his stomach. He whispered weakly that he had been hit four days ago and nothing had been done to him as yet. In the huge wound was a seething mass of living writhing insects. I weakened for a moment. I thought I knew just about everything, but I had never seen this before. I beckoned to an orderly. He came and took one look.

"Maggots," he said. "I'll get you a can of ether. That kills them." At first I thought I couldn't do it, but I did. The orderly explained that this was a natural, even a healthy symptom. I watched the squirming mass wither and die under the ether. When I removed them I saw that the wound was clean and fresh. These strange little organisms, it appears, eat away the decay and prevent infection of the blood stream. I soon learned to welcome the uncovering of these horrifying creatures, for often the removal of bandages revealed the hideous and hopeless color of gangrene.

A boy from Idaho, a big broad boy, had his head all bound up and the tag around his neck, put on at a dressing station, said: "Eyes shot away and both feet gone." I talked to him and patted him on the shoulder, assuring him that everything would be all right now. He moaned through the bandages that his head was splitting with pain. I gave him morphine. Suddenly aware of the fact that he had other wounds, he asked: "Sa-ay! what's the matter with my legs?" Reaching down to feel his legs before I could stop him, he uttered a heartbreaking scream. I held his hands firmly until the drug I had given him took effect.

August 8th

Have been working in the surgery with Dr. Le B. all day. I never thought I'd make it, but as there was no one else to fill in when Mlle. Ames, one of the older surgical nurses, col-

lapsed, I am quite proud of having been able to jump into her place at such short notice.

Dr. Le B. is too marvelous for words. He is not only a surgeon but an artist.

Lots of Americans wounded at Montdidier coming in.

Letter from Ted. He is still at Boulogne, training at the British Artillery School. I hope it ends before they get to him.

I had been longing to get into the surgery to help Dr. Le B. operate, but amateurs were not welcome in that sanctum. They had *real* nurses in there assisting the doctors. This day I noticed some confusion at the surgery door and found Dr. Le B. in despair. His nurse had fainted from exhaustion. All the other surgical nurses were busy and there was so much to be done. I asked him if I couldn't help him, but he waved me off impatiently. I begged him to let me try.

Did I, he asked somewhat wearily, know the French names for all the hundred and one little instruments he would have to use? I admitted I did not, even in English. Very well, then it was impossible! He shrugged and turned away. But I was not so easily discouraged. I followed him along the corridor and told him I would learn them. He looked at me a trifle witheringly; we had walked to the end of the corridor by this time. Learn them, he asked, when? He needed someone immediately. I would learn them immediately, I assured him. Would he help me make a list? I believe he was more curious than convinced, but he took me back to the surgery and went over the list with me. Rapidly I made notes and rough sketches of every instrument on the table. With this I went out to the vast park beyond the château where we had taken our walks, and tramped feverishly along the paths, memorizing the French names for the various kinds of knives, scissors, saws, pincers and dozens of little probes and mallets that are used for operating. Never had I studied a French lesson so avidly or so thoroughly. I went along the beautiful paths seeing nothing but little steel gee-gaws and babbling to myself like a lunatic.

Whether it was a miracle of devotion or emergency I do not know, but in less than two hours I reported to the surgery and found Dr.

Le B. He seemed surprised to see me back so soon, and asked if I was ready. I said I was. He rehearsed me over an instrument table, firing all those strange words at me bang-bang, like a machine gun. I gave him the instruments with trembling hands as quickly as I could find them. Of course, I made a few mistakes, but finally he beamed at me and said: *Bien, bien! Allons-y!* And we went to work.

I saw after that, all the surgery I ever want to see again. Difficult amputations, sutures, skull trapening, probing for bullets and shrapnel, blood transfusions, elementary plastics, spinal operations, and too many other kinds of human repair to list here.

Dr. Le B.'s hands, incased in rubber gloves, were swift and sure. He always worked with a cigarette hanging limply from the corner of his mouth. It was part of my job to keep lighting fresh ones for him. At first when the ashes fell into an open wound over which he was working, I asked him frantically what I should do about it. He went on calmly, muttering: *N'importe ça. C'est sterile.* It did not matter, the ashes were sterile. I have since been amused at the thought of so many men journeying through life sublimely unconscious of the fact that some part or another of their anatomy had once served as Dr. Le B.'s ash tray.

I worked in the surgery for several weeks while the regular nurse took a much-needed rest, and became very familiar with all the little instruments that were used in that department. I am afraid I was even guilty of trying to bring them into the conversation now and then, just to show how much I knew. What with a goodly supply of Army patter and slang, and a miscellany of surgical words at my tongue's tip, I was far better equipped, as far as French was concerned, for the war zone than for the drawing room. I learned this to my shame when I went on leave and visited some delightful but eminently conventional French friends. I could see, after a brief conversation, that they were often shocked. It was difficult for me to refrain from using such expressive words as *bobard* for tommyrot; *binette* for face; *Rosbif,* meaning a Britisher; *faire popote,* which meant eating together. *Rosalie* and *Berthe* were the *Boche* bayonet and gun, respectively. *Copain* meant buddy, and there were dozens of other choice and appropriate expressions, such as: *Quelle salade!* which meant, What a mess! a very useful and popular expression at the hospital; and there were so many others like it which I have since forgotten. Frankly, my conversation at that time was crippled without them.

One of the most striking things I remember about my apprenticeship in the surgery was the cutting open of a badly wounded Senegalese to probe for shrapnel. I shall never forget the sight of that expanse of ebony torso, gleaming against the white cover of the surgery table when suddenly the swift, sure stroke of a knife parted the black skin with a violent red-pink incision. I could not help being fascinated at the intense drama of the colors. It was like a great gash in an over-ripe watermelon and my somewhat callow imagination almost ran away with the idea that there would surely be little black seeds imbedded in the crimson flesh.

A peculiar case we had during this period was that of an American officer who had been shot in the hip. The bullet had struck a watch he carried in his hip pocket, shattered it, and propelled the pieces all the way down through his thigh to the knee. It took Dr. Le Brun over an hour to extract the fragments from the man's leg. Bits of crystal, tiny wheels, springs and hands, and all the minute mechanism of the watch were scattered about in the vicinity of the kneecap. This was an extremely difficult operation as well as an unusual one, and there is no doubt that the knee remained stiff for the rest of the officer's life. In spite of Le Brun's efforts to remove the fragments thoroughly, it was inevitable that in later years this man would be troubled by the occasional emergence of a spring, a wheel, or some such historical souvenir from goodness knows what part of his body.

August 14th

Am off surgical duty. Le B. has gone on leave. René, that fine young Alpine Chasseur who used to come to see Le B., is dead. I can hardly believe it. He was so alive, so fearless and unconquerable!

I promised Le B. that I would write to the girl in Dijon.

The circumstances of René's death come vividly to my mind. It was one of those strange fragments of melodrama which gave the war, as I look back on it, a note of fantastic unreality.

I was still in the surgery with Le B. and the cases were coming in thick and fast.

At the entrance of the operating room a doctor at the fluoroscope went over each patient thoroughly, back and front, from head to foot, and marked with a blue penciled cross the location of bullets or shrapnel or anything else that required removal or adjustment. The missile had usually penetrated in some unexpected direction from the actual wound and the blue crosses guided the surgeons in making incisions. Each new patient was wheeled to whichever surgeon happened to be free at the moment.

We had been working steadily for hours, I cannot recall how many, and the last case had been bandaged and sent on. There was hardly a moment's pause. Another was wheeled in instantly and transferred from the stretcher cart to an empty operating table. Ours was the nearest at hand, and so it was filled again. The anesthetist commenced automatically to apply the cone.

As I turned from hurriedly sterilizing the instruments, I saw Le B. bending over the figure before him, carefully studying its shattered face. The entire lower jaw had been shot away; the tongue was gone. As Le B. examined the hideous wound, he looked sharply at the head. I, too, had been gradually realizing that I was looking at someone I had seen before. Le B. glanced up at me quickly, his face ghastlier than it had ever been from fatigue. Our eyes met. We did not say a word, but I felt the uncontrollable tears stinging my lids and I turned away. The thick dark hair, the beautiful brow, the straight proud nose . . . and then nothing below it but a hideous cavernous wound, raw, jagged and bloody, where the laughing mouth had been. René!

Le B. ran his fingers distractedly through his hair, cursing bitterly in French. I went to him quickly with another pair of gloves. There were other wounds, too. Scores of blue crosses on the magnificent young body, and one leg completely crushed. With an effort I shook off the dizziness that threatened to overcome me and felt the pulse. It was still fairly strong. I watched Le B. attentively, waiting for his orders. Realizing his emotion, I poured him a glass of cognac and pressed it into his hand. He drank it mechanically. He was staring as if hypnotized at the man before him, bracing himself with his hands on the edge of the table.

My mind leaped to Dijon, to the girl who was waiting for René. I remembered the exquisite miniature and how I had imagined them together. . . . She is blonde like you, Mademoiselle. With so many freckles? In summer, many . . . but I adore every one of them! René, the ecstatic lover, the laughing warrior!

Le B. called for instruments and began working hurriedly. The usual cigarette was missing and he gritted his teeth instead. Every now and then he paused, staring into space. The man on the table groaned and stirred spasmodically. Perspiration dripped down Le B.'s face. He glanced up at the anesthetist. *"Encore,"* he said quietly. The orderly obeyed, placing the cone again over the broken face. *"Encore!"* Le B. said again. His voice had become harsh. There was a hollow silence as the indicator mounted. Le B. did not ask for any more instruments.

René never regained consciousness. Le B. worked no more that night. As he stripped off his gloves and started out of the surgery, he stopped and asked me to look up René's possessions and write to the girl in Dijon.

IX

It is slowing down again. The activity flows and ebbs like a tide. After an attack we are flooded with urgent cases, increasing as the drive pounds. So many we can hardly handle them. Then an ebb and gradually a lull, and then it starts all over again.

Letter from Ted. He will be in Paris in a few days and I am arranging leave to be with him. Wonder if he will still care. So much has happened. I feel changed. Told Le B. about going and he wanted to know when, and seemed to be considering getting off at the same time; so I told him I was going to meet a friend. He said: "A man friend, non? . . . I began to explain that it was someone I knew very well, had known for years, but I got rather tangled and I suppose my color gave me away as usual. Le B. looked at me seriously and suddenly suggested our taking a walk in the park.

We started off and he put my hand through his arm and held it very tight. We did not say much, but after a while he looked at me and said in French: "Do you know that you are a wonderful girl?" This was the first time Le B. had ever said anything like that to me, and my heart turned a back somersault. "Yes," he went on, "you can work like a man, and at the same time you are soft and sweet, and very brave. That is the best thing of all, to be brave." I couldn't think of anything else, so I said: "Thank you. I'm glad you think so well of me." Then he said: "What would you say if I told you that I love you very much?" I stared at him and must have looked silly standing there saying nothing. He took my hand and kissed it. Then he asked me if I loved this boy I was going to see in Paris. Frankly, at the moment I don't know whether I do or not. Ted seems so far away and long ago. Le B. has been part of my life for months. I have worked with him and worshiped him. So I said: "I don't know." He smiled and answered: "Never mind! We shall see when you return." Tucking my hand through his arm again, he turned and we started back.

When we got almost to the château, he stopped short and kissed me. I wish he hadn't. Have thought of nothing else all day. No, not even Ted.

September 3rd

Going on leave tomorrow. I have looked forward to seeing Ted for months, but now that I am really going to Paris, I don't want to go at all.

Le B. has given no sign that he feels any different than before. Wouldn't the girls be amazed if they knew! But I will not tell anyone. Le B. has guarded his feelings so discreetly that I shall keep the secret too.

Will work until four in the afternoon as usual, and then take a five o'clock train to Paris.

Have never been so mixed up in my emotions.

In this bewildered state, I went on leave. In four days I returned.

September 8th

Just back from Paris. It has been like a dream. Did it really happen? Four days have changed everything. I must get it all down, for I shall want to read this again and again when I am old. Not that I could ever forget, but it is so wonderful that I don't want one moment of it to slip out of my mind.

Ted met me at the train and I knew the minute he put his arms around me in the dismal old Gare du Nord that he is mine and I am his and, war or no war, we belong together.

He looked stunning in his uniform. He was tanned and toughened from the months of training. I wore my uniform, with the long blue cape and blue veil with white band. We looked and looked at each other like a pair of lunatics, laughing and asking silly questions that weren't what we wanted to say at all. Ted said: "Oh, my God, your hair is cut!" His face looked positively tragic.

There were so many things to talk about, with our hands clinging and our eyes glued on each other and . . . "Oh, darling, I'm so happy to see you. What do you mean by writing me such stingy letters? I almost went crazy thinking one of those damn French doctors had got you away from me. Let's get a taxi and ride around. Gosh, you look cute in that rig!"

We rode around; we walked around; we sat on benches in the Bois under the turning chestnut trees. War? Was there a war? Not just now, for us. There was only the joy of being together. We bought each other absurd presents, saying: "Wear this over your heart, darling. Carry this always and nothing can hurt you."

We seemed to feel, though we never admitted it to each other, that there was no time to waste, no certainty of peaceful years ahead. At any moment orders might come that would separate us. Beyond that we dared not think, I least of all.

Ted is concerned about the horrors I have seen. He exaggerates my courage and won't believe that I really don't mind. He insists that I am brave and noble and talks as though I were the only nurse in the whole war.

While we were walking, an air raid siren screamed a warning, but we paid no attention to it. We just kept wandering through the darkening streets hand in hand.

Suddenly we discovered we were hungry. We went to a bistro, the nearest we could find. Over the iron-topped table, to the tune of a mechanical piano jangling American jazz it was decided that I should take a small apartment.

We found one around the corner from the Chapelle de l'Expiatoire, *and I moved in with my little handbag that easily held what few things one needs in these convenient days of uniforms. It's really nice not to have a lot of dresses to bother about.*

Then we went out and stocked up on eggs and brioches *and some of the delicacies I had not tasted for so long. Ted got armfuls of flowers. We put them in just about everything, including the inevitable* pot-de-chambre *which no self-respecting French apartment is without.*

The windows of the stuffy little salon were heavily draped in red velour to match the red wall-paper and red plush chairs, and I suppose it was quite awful, but I shall always remember it as the most beautiful place I have ever seen.

Toward midnight the concierge came to the door and discreetly suggested that if Monsieur intended to spend the night, perhaps she had better bring up more linen. But I told her Monsieur was staying at the Crillon, thank you; news which she received with evident disappointment. The French love romance and I am sure she went away sadly deploring our apparent lack of it.

What heavenly days! How grand to wake up in the morning with nothing to do! Ted usually arrived before I was dressed and we shouted through the door, making our plans for the day. Then out we went, arm in arm. We couldn't pass a beggar or a child without giving him a coin or a sweet. We bought flowers from every flower girl we met and gave them away to bewildered strangers.

One night we went to the Casino de Paris and heard an attractive young poilu in uniform sing naughty French songs. His name is Chevalier, and everyone seems to be crazy about him.

We found out-of-the-way restaurants where we wouldn't run into people we knew, and danced blissfully among the poilus and their poules, all of us smiling at each other, feeling the kinship of lovers.

We went to Père la Chaise and reverently placed a wreath of everlasting on the grave of Abélard and Héloïse.

As the days passed, it became more and more difficult to turn our minds away from the fear that when Ted got back to the hotel there would be word waiting that would separate us. And each evening we celebrated the fact that orders had not come. My heart almost stops every time I think of Ted going up to the line. He is like all the other Americans; he doesn't know what he will get into. He drove me frantic by saying he hoped to God he wouldn't be stuck off in some dull sector. He wants action.

Well, he's getting it. The orders came on the fourth day, and his battalion was ordered directly to the front. We looked up Fer-en-Tardenois on the map. That is where he is meeting his regiment. It is not far from the line.

I saw him off. Then I went back to the little red plush apartment and cried. Brave and noble, am I? Finally gathered up my few belongings and came back to the hospital.

I suppose all this has been said and done before, but it is new to me and I know I shall never live those four days again. Perhaps it is all I will ever have. I must not let myself think that.

We plan to be married the minute all this hubbub is over.

This entry omits the true picture of Paris at that time. I saw it again, shortly afterward — without benefit of rose-tinted glasses, but with my heart full and frightened.

It was a somber, subdued Paris, a ghostly city. There were no lights at night except faint glimmers far apart along the deserted streets, and they were carefully covered by umbrella-like shades. All activities were conducted by women, aged men, and *blessés,* mutilated men who limped about on crutches or served one slowly in the restaurants, not yet accustomed to the loss of an arm or hand.

Occasionally one saw a man walking tragically apart, wearing a flesh-colored mask over his face, held on with elastic behind the ears, some covering the face completely, and some only partially hiding disfigured features.

Long lines of black-clad women, swathed in heavy crêpe veils and wearing the dull beads that denote mourning, waited at the supply stations for their daily ration of bread. Women swept the streets; drove taxis; sold newspapers; delivered mail. There was no sugar for afternoon tea, no butter for morning rolls. Hardly any men in the streets except soldiers, officers and Government officials. What foreign women one saw in public places were in uniform; canteen workers, Red Cross nurses, ambulance drivers or secretaries. From the time of her arrival in France until after the Armistice was signed, no girl or woman connected with the service ever appeared in anything but her uniform, of which she was tremendously proud. Even at dances at the Inter-Allied Club, or an evening at the Folies Bergères, there would not be an evening gown in sight. Only dark dresses, tailored suits or uniforms. Whatever gaiety one saw in Paris at this time was high-keyed, unreal, and never quite covered the grim undertone of tragedy.

After my romantic leave, I resumed my life at the hospital.

September 11th

Told Le B. about Ted today. He wished me happiness and added: "If anything ever happens to change your decision, will you let me know?"

But I know that nothing will ever change my decision.

Ted gave me a little silver charm to put on my identification bracelet. It has engraved on it: Plus que hier, moins que demain. *That's how I feel too. I love him more every day.*

Yet I feel miserable, what with Le B. being so nice about it and my worry over Ted haunting me night and day. So many Americans are coming in. Every one of them seems another Ted to me now.

September 15th

Went to the funeral of four Americans in the little church-yard. Liz and I felt these were our own boys and we could not let them be buried in foreign soil alone; so we went.

I read the tags: Donnelly, Goldfarb, Wendel, and Auerbach.

It was terribly sad and I wept so hard that Liz whispered: "For heaven's sake stop, Red, or you'll get me started!' But I couldn't stop.

What's the sense of it? Why did they have to be killed before they had even begun to live?

No more funerals for me. I can't get those four pine boxes out of my mind.

It was such a beautiful clear day with meadow-larks singing over head. There were four army *caissons,* each pulled by two men, each with a coffin on it, covered by an American flag. We followed the procession as it creaked slowly along the rough road and turned in at the cemetery gate.

There was a yawning trench in the dark earth, and the men who had pulled the *caissons* unloaded the boxes and placed them an even distance apart beside the freshly dug grave. Ropes were knotted around each box. An orderly unfastened the flags so that they could be pulled away. The men heaved and tugged. The ropes crunched on the crude edges of the wood. One by one the boxes were lowered. A wizened old padre intoned the service in a mechanical drone; something about the mercy and goodness of God. He had done it so many times that his voice was expressionless. I watched the boxes go down and reach the bottom. Then the spades flew and the black dirt thudded on the wood, crumbling, quickly covering the coffins.

The men who filled up the trench had grim, stony faces. When the last few spadefuls of earth had fallen on the long grave, one of them who appeared to be in charge drew some papers from his pocket, took four empty beer bottles from one of the *caissons* and, after examining the slips, inserted one in each bottle and thrust them neck down into the earth above each coffin. He seemed to know what he was doing, but I wonder now, as I wondered then, if he really got the identification slips in their right places.

We all stood at attention as the bugle played taps. Taps! My thoughts were so poignant I remember them well. Taps forever! Good-by to youth and all the dreams they had. Dreams like Ted's and mine.

I understood now why they had been so strict about not wanting us in the hospital service if we had a relative or a fiancé in the war. My efficiency was considerably impaired by my worry over Ted. It required enormous effort to perform tasks that had been easy before. Every new case made me quiver at the possibility that these things might happen to Ted. Then one day I received a telegram.

September 20th

Ted has been wounded. At Fismes. He says not bad, nothing to worry about. But that is what they always say.

Am trying to get away and Le B. is helping me arrange it, bless his dear heart.

Oh, God, please . . . please!

That trip to Paris was too painful to describe. Every stop seemed an hour long; yet I dreaded to arrive. What would I find? How could I bear it? The fact that he had been taken directly to Paris might mean that it really was not too bad.

My heavy feet stumbled up the hospital steps and I finally arrived in the ward. I found Ted with a fractured leg and his left arm suspended in a frame. The first thing I said to him — and he never did let me forget it — was: "Oh, darling, thank God you're not hurt!" Not *hurt!* He looked deeply offended. To his way of thinking, he was very badly hurt indeed. My words must have sounded heartless, but at the hospital we were accustomed to regarding the head, chest and body wounds as the most serious. When I saw that he had arm and leg fractures I was so relieved I forgot to consider his feelings in the matter. However, I explained remorsefully what I'd meant, and one of the nurses considerately drew a screen about us so I could make up for my careless greeting.

I could stay only a few hours and returned to my post thankful that Ted would be out of the line of fire for some time. Meanwhile, perhaps it would end.

October 4th

Foch is a terrific general. Imagine having taken a quarter of a million prisoners! Well, if they are all as unpleasant as some I have seen, he is welcome to them.

We are rushed again. All beds full. A big drive is on, with loads of Americans wounded. I am glad Ted is not in the thick of it.

October 5th

Big news! Emilie, our little lost sheep, is going to be married tomorrow.

One of the cooks has fallen so hard for that baby and its mother that he is going to make an honest pair of them.

Mme de R. acts as though it were a personal triumph, and is making all the arrangements. Everyone is contributing something toward a dot and a trousseau for Emilie, and if Mme de R. doesn't think the contribution is large enough (especially from the doctors), she nags until she gets more. Really she is a brick! I am giving one of my best nighties and five dollars. Emilie struts around like a little pouter pigeon. She is getting prettier every day, and as for the baby, I don't blame the cook for wanting it. I'd like to have it myself. It laughs and gurgles and eats and sleeps, and isn't a bit of trouble to anyone. I've never heard it cry.

Our so-called lost sheep was married, with a veil and all. Mme de R. saw to that. Of course the veil was made of mosquito netting, but with real French artistry. Mme de R. made a bandeau of one of her best lace handkerchiefs and Emilie was a lovely bride. As for the groom, he literally shone with soap, water, hair oil, and happiness. They were married in the chapel of the château by the same priest who conducted the burials; and Mme de R. in spite of her elation up to this point, ran true to form and cried at the wedding. Dr. Clèment was the best man, and everyone who could sneak off, managed to get to the chapel for a glimpse of Emilie. The bride and groom were given two days' leave and they went gaily off in one of the supply *camions* to the cook's home town, Chantilly, for their honeymoon, baby and all.

X

November 6th

The fighting continues near Sedan. I am on duty in the Salle de Mort, a ward where the dying cases are quartered. They are there only a few days and are replaced constantly. Seven Americans in the ward now from the Meuse-Argonne battle.

One in particular, Charley Whiting, has won our hearts so completely that we dread the end to come. He is a young Sergeant in the 2nd Engineers, shot through the spine and totally paralyzed. Even now, with his spirit almost over the brink, one can see what a wonderful boy he must have been. He is so lovable; clean and sweet as spring water. He cannot speak more than one or two words at a time, in a gasping whisper, but manages to say: Thank, you, and smiles with his eyes whenever anything is done for him. He cannot move a muscle except his eyes and two fingers of one hand. He lies all day and all through the long night in exactly the same position. We do not dare to move him. We all love him so much that we are trying to keep him with us as long as possible.

I can imagine Charley in all his beauty and youthful strength, laughing, teasing, singing, marching with his helmet cocked over one ear. . . . "Hey, where is all this trouble anyway? . . ."

Today he tried to say something and I bent down to listen. He said: "My mother . . ." It is getting more and more difficult for him to speak. I asked if he meant that he had not written to her for quite some time. His face relaxed with relief. His eyes said yes, and with the two fingers he can still move he motioned toward his pocketbook. I got it for him and found his mother's name and address, and told him I would write to her.

Tears came to his eyes for the first time. They were not for himself but for her. I patted his hand and busied myself, fighting back my own tears.

My heart is sick over the thought of the letter I must write.
What can I say? How can I say it?

In they came, young and shattered. Out they went, covered with a sheet, to the chill cellar beyond which had once stored provisions for the banquet tables of the château. Then on to the churchyard.

We tried to write to as many of the American families as we could, but there were so many. Most of the messages had to go through regular War Department channels which meant weeks of delay and anxiety across the ocean and then the terse, regretful announcement, typewritten and final.

November 8th

More and more Americans in the death ward. Gas cases are terrible. They cannot breathe lying down or sitting up. They just struggle for breath, but nothing can be done . . . their lungs are gone . . . literally burnt out. Some with their eyes and faces entirely eaten away by the gas, and bodies covered with first degree burns. We try to relieve them by pouring oil on them. They cannot be bandaged or even touched. We cover them with a tent of propped-up sheets. Gas burns must be agonizing because usually the other cases do not complain even with the worst of wounds. But gas cases invariably are beyond endurance and they cannot help crying out.

One boy today, screaming to die. The entire top layer of skin burned from his face and body. I gave him an injection of morphine. He was wheeled out just before I came off duty. . . .

Yesterday an English boy in the fracture ward went insane. He tried to choke one of the English nurses. She struggled with him and the orderlies rushed over and pinned him down. Poor kid! They had to put him in a strait-jacket. I wonder what will happen to him.

He was one of our best patients, a brilliant and amusing youngster who had come straight from Cambridge.

I am feeling tired and ill. When will it end?

November 10th

Charley died this morning. I held his hand as he went and could not keep back the tears. Near the end he saw me crying and patted my hand with his two living fingers to comfort me. I cannot describe that boy's sweetness. He took part of my heart with him. Everybody around the place was in tears.

Just after he went someone came into the ward and said: "Armistice! The staff cars have just passed by the gate on their way to Senlis to sign an Armistice!"

What a time and place to come in shouting about an Armistice! I said: "Sh! Sh!"

There is no armistice for Charley or for any of the others in that ward. One of the boys began to sob. I went and talked soothingly to him, but what could I say, knowing he would die before night?

Well, it's over. I have to keep telling myself, it's over, it's over, it's over.

But there is still that letter to write to Charley's mother. I can hear commotion and shouting through the hospital as I write this. The chapel bell is ringing wildly.

I am glad it is over, but my heart is heavy as lead. Must write that letter.

One of the girls came looking for me. They have opened champagne for the staff in the dining hall. I told her to get out.

Can't seem to pull myself together.

We were dismissed that day. The hospital would be evacuated and closed. Next day the world would know that the war was over, and the regular nurses would carry on where we left off. I felt numb, bewildered. Only then did the enormous crime of the whole thing begin to come home to me. All very well to celebrate, I thought, but what about Charley? All the Charlies? What about Donnelly, Goldfarb, Wendel, Auerbach? And René? And the hundreds, thousands, of others.

I finished the letter to Charley's mother, packed my few belongings and got ready to leave. Leave, for where? Home? I felt a sudden shyness about returning home. I dreaded the curious eyes and eager questions. They would make a fuss. I knew that from the letters and newspaper clippings I had received. I shrank from the prospect of honors I neither wanted nor deserved. How could they know what *real* bravery, *real* heroism, was? I had seen it and wanted no chatter about it over teacups and cocktail glasses.

When the time came to leave I went to the churchyard. Le B. went with me. He held my hand and did not say a word as we looked over the rows and rows of crosses. I was beyond feeling anything except the numbness of grief.

I went to my last ward to say good-by to some of my favorites. I found a boy from Arkansas, who had been totally blinded and had been wonderfully plucky and cheerful about it, sitting with a letter in his hands. The bandage around his eyes was soaked with tears. I sat on his bed and covered his hand with mine. What was the trouble? Could I do anything for him? He handed me the letter and asked me to read it to him again. I did. It contained the happy news of the birth of a boy to his young wife. She had not yet had word of his injury and her letter bubbled with joy and anticipation: He is so like you! I am praying every minute that the war will end for I can hardly wait to see your dear face when you see him . . .

What could I say? My heart overflowed. All I could think of was: I hope he will grow up to be as brave and wonderful as his father. One always managed to think of banalities at the right moment. I said them all, but the boy's silence and the tear-soaked bandage were mute testimony to the comfortless anguish of his spirit.

We all gathered in the study and the hospital chief made a speech, thanking the unit for having served France. It was a jumble of empty words to me that day. We shook hands with all the French nurses and doctors and hoped we would see each other again, and exchanged addresses. But there were very few of them I ever saw or heard from again.

I went immediately to Paris, where I spent a great deal of time with Ted. He looked very white and thin, and was limping around on a cane, with one arm in a sling. Finally he was sent back to America on a hospital ship. I joined the American Red Cross, and divided my time between nursing and shopping for my trousseau until my turn came to be sent home.

Many were wounded on the day of the Armistice, before the news reached remote sectors. And for days afterward the hospital trains came into Paris loaded with crippled men.

While in Paris, I received a letter from Indiana, forwarded to me from the château. It was from Charley's mother:

Fairfield, Indiana,
November 26th, 1918.

Dear Friend:

Thank you for writing me about my boy. It was a sad blow, but I realize how fortunate I was to have more than the short message which came from the War Department a week later.

Your letter has been my only comfort in these terrible days. I can understand your fondness for Charles. Everyone here is saddened by his death. I still cannot believe I will never see him again.

He was all I had. His father died when he was fourteen and he has worked ever since to help me.

His employers were holding his position open for him.

He had a girl he loved dearly and they were planning to be married. We try to comfort each other, but all we can say is how brave he was, and thank God there was someone good and kind to take care of him to the last.

I have read your letter over and over. It seems to be all I have left of him. I showed it to Mr. Petrie, the editor of our paper, and he asked permission to print it. I am enclosing the clipping. It was right on the front page and I was so proud of all the things you said about my boy. It means so much to me to know he said Mother *at the end.*

Perhaps you will have a son of your own some day. Then you will know how much they mean to us. I can only pray God there will never be another dreadful war like this has been.

My heart is too full to write more. Thank you, thank, you, dear friend. May God bless and keep you.

Ever your grateful

Emma B. Whiting.

I returned to America, and the day after my arrival, Ted and I were married.

Now the world is once again beating the drums of war. To my son Coco, his friends and their mothers I offer this simple record of the dark caravan that winds endlessly through the memory of my youth.

———————

About the 2011 Edition

An unprepared nurse from the United States volunteering in World War I France shares her diary and later reflections of the horrific and poignant events of 1918, and in the process reveals more about the fascinating people and times, and especially herself, than she apparently realized even in writing it. Presented to modern readers with a new Foreword by Elizabeth Townsend Gard. Includes contemporary photographs of World War I medics serving in France.

Elizabeth Townsend Gard is an associate professor of law at Tulane University in New Orleans, where she specializes in intellectual property, copyright, and legal history. She co-directs the Tulane Center for Intellectual Property Law and Culture. In addition to two law degrees from the University of Arizona, Townsend Gard earned her M.A. and Ph.D. in Modern European History from the University of California at Los Angeles, where her research explored World War I narratives and novelizations of the War to End All Wars.

www.quidprobooks.com

7968900R0

Made in the USA
Charleston, SC
26 April 2011